A Beginner's Guide to

PRAYER

*The Orthodox Way
to Draw Closer to God*

by Father Michael Keiser

Conciliar Press
Ben Lomond, California

A BEGINNER'S GUIDE TO PRAYER:
The Orthodox Way to Draw Closer to God
© Copyright 2003 by Michael Keiser

Published by   Conciliar Press
                P.O. Box 76
                Ben Lomond, California 95005-0076

Printed in the United States of America

ISBN 1-888212-64-0

Manufactured under the direction of Double Eagle Industries.
For manufacturing details, call 888-824-4344
or e-mail to info@publishingquest.com

Contents

Chapter 1

Why Should I Pray?

Seven times a day I praise You.
—Psalm 119:164

The other Sunday, a friend of mine who is a pastor took an informal survey of his congregation during the homily. "How many of you struggle with your prayer life?" he asked. Every hand in this parish of nearly three hundred shot up! The priest admitted that prayer was his own greatest spiritual struggle. The fact is, practicing effective prayer is like fighting on the front lines in a war. Our greatest challenge is to pray!

This is an interesting time to be Orthodox. Our secular world provides little certainty for people's lives, and the Orthodox faith issues an unchanging message of truth and stability. Orthodox Christianity may be the last firm footing on which to stand, yet it would be fair to say that very few Orthodox Christians are aware of the depth and richness of the Church's spiritual tradition when it comes to *personal* devotion. We Orthodox are big on externals. Our liturgical worship is a drama of striking beauty and color, of scent and sound. But besides being beautiful, icons, vestments, chanting, and incense together constitute an important statement about God. He has created us as physical beings in a material world, and we approach Him using the elements of that material world. The way in which we Orthodox worship involves all of our senses and physical nature, so that we may respond to God with all of our being—our bodies as well as our minds and souls.

However, there is something else that is as essential to our spiritual growth as outward worship, and that is personal prayer. Anyone who wants to grow closer to God must develop a disciplined prayer life.

✦ What Is Prayer? ✦

Public worship and personal prayer are the twin support beams of the spiritual life for any believer. All our growing will take place within the framework they provide. But they are not the same thing, and they are not interchangeable.

Certainly we pray when we come to church, but we do other things as well—we sing, we learn, we offer. Worship is what we do as a group, when we gather as Christ's Body. The prayer that is offered by the Church is a united offering of prayer, "on behalf of all and for all," to the Father, in Christ, by the Holy Spirit.

✦ One-on-One ✦

Personal prayer is just that, personal and individual. It is my own personal conversation with God, in which no one else will be involved. In personal prayer I will pray *for* others, but not *with* others.

Jesus' teaching about prayer makes it clear: "But you, when you pray, go into your room, and when you have shut your door, pray to your Father who *is* in the secret *place*; and your Father who sees in secret will reward you openly" (Matthew 6:6).

Personal prayer is our own private time with our Father. Everyone feels the need for a little personal attention at times, and in prayer we get that; but it never replaces our worship in church. The oneness of being in the Body of Christ, united in faith and love with other believers, is both glorious and necessary. But an individual relationship with God is just as important. In order to be a complete Christian one must relate to the members of the Body of Christ together, *and* relate to God as a person. St. John of Kronstadt (1829–1908) wrote, "Why is it necessary to pray at home, and to attend divine services in church? Well, why is it necessary for you to eat and drink, to take exercise, or to work every day? In order to support the life of the body and strengthen it." Worship and prayer are the food and drink, the work and workout, of our life with God.

Your relationship with a personal God is what private prayer is all about. There are many things required for our growth, such as reading, study, and good works. But they will bear no real fruit unless they are supported by the life of worship and prayer.

❧ Good Tools for an Effective Job ❦

Why should we be concerned about being effective? Because we do not want to waste time when it comes to something as important as prayer. God has given us a job to do, and the job description is a dandy. "Therefore you shall be perfect, just as your Father in heaven is perfect" (Matthew 5:48). What could be simpler? We just have to be perfect!

If we are to meet such a challenge, we cannot waste time spinning our wheels. We must do the most efficient job of praying that we can. Being concerned about efficiency does not mean only making decisions about style and technique. We will deal with those things in the course of this book, but to be effective we must also be concerned about results. Is your prayer life helping you to reach the goal of Christian perfection? If not, then it may be worse than no prayer at all, because *it is a waste of time*! Prayer is not an end in itself, but a means by which we draw closer to God.

Jesus said, "If you abide in Me, and My words abide in you, you will ask what you desire, and it shall be done for you. By this My Father is glorified, that you bear much fruit" (John 15:7, 8). Our Christian growth can be measured, just as you would measure the quality of a vine by the fruit it bears. Our grapes are our thoughts and actions. Are they like Christ's thoughts and actions? Are we becoming more Christlike? The more Christlike in action we become, the more fruit we will bear.

Being concerned about the effectiveness of our prayer also prevents, or at least helps us avoid, misdirection, and it allows us to correct mistakes as they occur. The problems we will encounter will not be new problems; untold numbers of people have faced them before us. We have good directions: in Holy Scripture, and in the writings of holy people who have cultivated God's Word abiding in them and have borne much fruit. We call these holy persons "saints." They are our fathers and mothers in the Faith, and their experience can prevent us from fumbling around if we pay attention to it.

❧ *The Love Connection* ❧

Americans are practical people. We like to know what is involved before committing ourselves to a program. It only makes sense to do things this way. Jesus certainly expressed this idea when He said, "For which of you, intending to build a tower, does not sit down first and count the cost, whether he has *enough* to finish *it?*" (Luke 14:28). So we need to count the cost. Why bother with the effort of a disciplined prayer life at all?

There are several possible answers to the question, but I find two to be persuasive: We pray *as a response* to love, and we pray *in order* to love. "Beloved, let us love one another, for love is of God; and everyone who loves is born of God and knows God. . . . In this is love, not that we loved God, but that He loved us and sent

His Son *to be* the propitiation for our sins" (1 John 4:7, 10).

God always takes the first step! We do not have to worry about getting in touch with Him, because He has already established contact with us by sending His Son to die for us. God is the primary Lover of the creation and everything in it—the One who sweeps us off our feet the first time we really encounter Him. And He does this not so much by what He does as by who He is.

Remember when you fell in love? Everyone has done so at some time or another. It may have been with your second-grade teacher or a high-school football star. Your new love probably did nothing in particular to get your attention, except show up! But when you discovered that person, you did not know what had hit you.

That is the kind of Lover our God is. He doesn't try to grab our attention with fancy clothes or a flashy car. The approach is more subtle. He is just here, always here. He introduces His presence into your life, and then one day you wake up with the knowledge that you cannot live without Him! He is the Great Lover, and when you are on the receiving end of His love, you just cannot help but respond. Prayer is our act of response. When we love someone, we want to be with him, do things with him, and respond to him.

Please notice the words "act" and "do." For Christians, love is action, not feeling. Christian love is not the warm rush of desire and joy that can be experienced in a love affair, political rally, or charismatic power meeting. That is romanticism, *not* Christianity. So responding to God with warm feelings is not what prayer should be about. As we shall see, the Orthodox tradition is very cautious about such things.

Love experienced on the deep level of reality results in a conscious decision to act toward someone in a caring way and to communicate with that person. So God acts by sending His Son, the Eternal Word, to us. This is the ultimate declaration of love. We respond to the sending of His Word with our words. We pray.

✦ *The Act of Loving* ✦

Prayer is more than just our response to the way God loves us. It is part of how we love Him. Love breaks down separation because we want to be one with the person we love. If we love God, we want to become one with Him. St. Dimitri of Rostov wrote, "No unity with God is possible without an exceeding great love." Loving and joining go together.

But you cannot become one with someone if you never talk to him. You cannot be in love with someone you do not know. Genuine lovers are always discovering things about each other. The more you know about the one you love, the more you will be in love with him.

Our relationship with God is like that, and it is not hard to understand what happens. In order to love Him, we have to trustingly open ourselves to Him, and He will open Himself to us. We become one with our Lover. "Draw near to God and He will draw near to you" (James 4:8). He already knows about us (He did create us, remember), but He will open Himself to us so that we can learn as much as possible about Him. This does not mean that we will learn everything there is to know about God, but we will learn all that we can possibly absorb. We can ask no more of any lover.

Our love will express itself in a desire for knowledge and union. Prayer is the way we express our desire and the way we achieve it. To understand the need for prayer, we must realize how much we need a personal relationship with God. Prayer is the encounter between two loving persons seeking to become one: God in us, and we in Him. "My beloved *is* mine, and I *am* his" (Song of Solomon 2:16).

God walks among the hills and valleys of His creation with something in His glance that pulls us toward Him. "You have ravished my heart . . . / With one *look* of your eyes" (Song of Solomon 4:9). Do not be afraid to respond to God. Never be afraid to love Him! He is calling for us: "Rise up, my love, my fair one, / And come away" (Song of Solomon 2:10).

What are you waiting for? Start to pray!

Chapter 2

Beginning Basics

Who is there that does not know the ordinary hours of prayer to be the third, the sixth and the ninth, together with the morning and the evening.
—St. Jerome

To construct a good prayer life, we must follow some simple rules. These rules help us to avoid mistakes and wasted effort. Even if you are an experienced prayer warrior, it helps to review the basics in order to avoid falling into bad habits.

The first thing you must accept is the necessity of discipline and training. There is a temptation to think discipline might hamper freedom or quench the spirit—and there will be lots of people who will try to tell you just that—but it's not true. The fact is that freedom of any kind is impossible without discipline. There is no such thing as unlimited freedom, because what we do affects other people and *their* freedom. Discipline is the self-restraint that we use to prevent hurting others, and ourselves, as we exercise freedom. And discipline is godly. "Furthermore, we have had human fathers who corrected *us*, and we paid *them* respect. Shall we not much more readily be in subjection to the Father of spirits and live?" (Hebrews 12:9).

When Jesus taught His followers about prayer, He was giving them a discipline they could use to pray effectively. By using these disciplines as a proper foundation from the start, you can avoid many problems that will come up later.

There are going to be many pitfalls that we must avoid, and some of them will seem rather small. But the devil is in the details. "Be sober, be vigilant; because your adversary the devil walks about like a roaring lion, seeking whom he may devour" (1 Peter 5:8). Satan loves to mess with our spiritual lives. One of the best ways he has to do this is to slip something small past us, hoping we will not notice. Most of us would recognize a major attack—demons crying out in the middle of the night tend to get a person's attention. The devil is not stupid. He knows it is easier to trip us up with a lot of small, frustrating difficulties that can add up to one big problem. So, in self-defense, we must pay attention to detail.

Now, having said that, don't become paranoid every time the phone rings during your prayer time, assuming that it is an incoming call from the nether regions. The Apostle Peter said, "Be vigilant," not, "Be crazy." Many Christians become subtly fixated on evil, and they end up attributing every problem in life to the devil. These people are convinced they are under constant attack. They feel like General Custer at the Little Big Horn with every Indian in the world coming at him. When you feel that way, Satan has scored. You can become so concerned about beating off attacks that you never get anything positive done. You must have a sense of discernment and proportion.

Remember, we are not in this alone. Jesus taught, "If anyone loves Me, he will keep My word; and My Father will love him, and We will come to him and make Our home with him" (John 14:23). Prayer is not the same as talking to ourselves! One of the obstacles to true prayer is assuming that it depends solely on our efforts. Prayer also involves the big Three—Father, Son, and Holy Spirit, who are not just the object of our prayer, but its content and source as well.

The object of our praying is the Father. The Son is our access to Him: "No one comes to the Father except through Me" (John 14:6). The power for our praying comes from the Holy Spirit, the Spirit of truth who was sent to us by Jesus from the Father: "But when the Helper comes, whom I shall send to you from the Father . . ." (John 15:26). We have a helper in our struggles. "Likewise the Spirit also helps in our weaknesses. For we do not know what we should pray for as we ought, but the Spirit Himself makes intercession for us with groanings which cannot be uttered" (Romans 8:26).

Prayer does not begin in us. Believing that we succeed in praying because of what we do is a sin of pride. Although we are concerned about discipline and method, we must always remember that all true prayer is prompted by the Holy Spirit, who is leading us in Christ to the Father.

Thank God for that! We need not worry about what to say, because the Spirit will tell us. He can even take our prayer beyond that of spoken words and intercede for us "with groanings which cannot be uttered." So you can relax a bit. Let the Holy Trinity go to work. Prayer will take a lot of effort on your part, but you will have all the help you could ever need.

❧ Let's Get Started ❦

When starting any project, it helps to read the instructions. In this case, our instructions are recorded in the Apostle Matthew's Gospel: "And when you pray, you shall not be like the hypocrites. For they love to pray standing in the synagogues and on the corners of the streets, that they may be seen by men. Assuredly, I say to you, they have their reward. But you, when you pray, go into your room, and when you have shut your door, pray to your

Father who *is* in the secret *place*; and your Father who sees in secret will reward you openly" (Matthew 6:5, 6).

The fact that Jesus gave special instructions to His disciples about prayer is another indication that prayer is meant to be structured and disciplined. Jesus never said, "Wing it, guys, and let the Spirit flow." In addition, the first direction Jesus gave emphasizes how personal and private our prayer life should be. We are not to be seen by others. No one is supposed to know we are being pious. On the contrary, we are told we must withdraw to a private place—our "room."

There are several reasons for this instruction from Jesus. First, prayer is, in one sense, an inward journey to encounter the Trinity, who is dwelling within us. As St. Macarius of Egypt wrote, "The heart is a small vessel, but all things are contained in it; God is there, the angels are there, and there also is life and the kingdom, the heavenly cities and the treasures of grace." Crowded, isn't it?

Prayer is our entry into the reality of an encounter with the Holy Trinity. Now obviously, this is going to take all our attention, so we have to start by shutting out distractions. WARNING! Satan is in the distraction business, with a full line of products guaranteed to keep us from paying attention to the task at hand. And even if, as we have noted, the distractions don't necessarily come from him, they are *still* distractions. So we need to shut the door on them.

✦ *Setting the Stage* ✦

Every Orthodox home should have an icon "corner"—one particular place where icons, a cross, a Bible, and a prayerbook are kept, and where it is possible to pray without distraction. (The icon corner can also double as a place for family devotions, which are not the same thing as personal prayer.) Our icon corner should be as quiet and undisturbed as possible, so that we can concentrate.

Try to pray in the same place as much as possible. Sanctifying a particular place with regular prayer can make it easier to "get in the mood." There will be many times when we will need the refuge of a holy place, and places that have been sanctified by previous prayer become settings for divine encounter. When you are in those places, the desire and need for prayer will come to mind.

If you happen to be in church, you can certainly say your prayers there. A holier place could not be found! I once had a parishioner who stopped saying prayers in church completely after studying Matthew 6:5, 6, where Jesus speaks of withdrawing into your closet. There is no need to be that literal! But Jesus knew that most of us would not live in a church building, so He instructed us to set aside a holy place at home.

In addition to praying in a regular *place*, we should pray at a regular *time*. This discipline was rooted in the Old Testament Temple and continues in the Church. "The third, sixth, and ninth hours divide the day into even spaces of time, and are therefore allotted to prayer: that while we are intent on other business, and may forget our duties toward God, the very hour when it comes may put us in mind thereof." So wrote St. Isidore in the second century. If prayer becomes a godly routine (rather than just a pious habit), our subconscious mind will often remind us of what we should be doing.

St. Isidore mentions three times a day, which were traditionally regarded as being in addition to morning and evening prayers. The hours mentioned correspond to nine A.M., noon, and three P.M. These times for prayer (morning, nine A.M., noon, three P.M., and evening) were the basis on which monastic worship developed, but they were also times of private devotion during the day.

The same hours of prayer were observed in the Temple in Jerusalem, and after the Resurrection, the Christian community in Jerusalem continued to keep them. "Now Peter and John went up together to the temple at the hour of prayer, the ninth *hour*" (Acts 3:1). Disciplined prayer is rooted in the Bible!

Unfortunately, our modern way of life tends to be less tolerant of "time-outs." If you work outside your home, your coffee breaks may not coincide with the prayer hours. So you will need to choose times of prayer that fit your particular rhythm of life. Choose times when you know you can concentrate.

For example, I don't do mornings. Trying to say my prayers at seven A.M. would not work: I would have to put more effort into just staying awake than into praying. Likewise, a parent who has to get children off to school may have to postpone prayer until the kiddies are gone. It is hard to fix your attention on God when your six-year-old is experimenting with cooking Froot Loops in the toaster.

Believe it or not, flexibility is essential to good discipline. The reason so many Christians have a negative attitude toward disciplined prayer is that they see it as being too rigid. Genuine discipline always has room for change, when necessary. There will be things such as work, school, or family that will sometimes get in the way of your praying in the same place at the same time. There is no need to throw in the towel. Rules should never be elevated to the level of dogma. Rigidity hurts, but reasonable discipline helps. If it is necessary to revise our rule of prayer—temporarily or for a longer period—we should not be afraid to do so. If necessary, we can pray at any time in any place.

✤ *Home Is Where the Heart Is* ✤

There will be occasions when you cannot withdraw to a private place for prayer. It would be a bit obvious to keep popping into the broom closet at work, and Jesus has already told us not to draw attention to ourselves. When location is a problem, we need to enter the room of our heart. This means withdrawing spiritually into our "own space," shutting out the interference from the world around us. This is difficult, but the saints did it, and the saints are people just like us, not a group of semi-divine beings. The saints just took their job very seriously. To succeed you will need good concentration, spiritual strength, and lots of practice.

Try a little experiment. Sit back and concentrate on one thought, and only one thought, for ten to fifteen minutes. Your goal is to allow nothing else to settle into your mind. Hard, isn't it? We are not accustomed to concentrating on one thing to the exclusion of everything else. And there are few places really free of distraction. Even elevators have music piped into them, to keep us from being alone with ourselves. So most of us are out of practice in the fine art of concentration. But with work, it can get easier.

First, you will have to remind yourself over and over that you are *always* in the presence of God. There will be many times when it may not seem like it, but He is always with you. Just as real is the presence of the angelic hosts and the saints. "Therefore we also, since we are surrounded by so great a cloud of witnesses, let us lay aside every weight, and the sin which so easily ensnares *us*, and let us run with endurance the race that is set before us" (Hebrews 12:1).

Regular prayer in a regular place, if at all possible, will bring this heavenly reality home to you. But until you can establish the necessary strength and concentration to withdraw into your hearts, I would suggest not trying. You will only become frustrated.

Start with regular prayers at your icon corner, even if it doesn't seem like much now. With experience and regular contact with heaven, your strength to push distraction aside will grow.

Establishing a regular time and place for prayer is the first step toward what is called a "rule of life." This rule provides the structure and discipline that makes effective praying—as well as other aspects of our piety, like fasting, spiritual reading, and almsgiving—possible. The word "rule" comes from the Latin word *regula*, which means that ascetic discipline should be thought of as a regular part of our daily lives, rather than some unyielding plan imposed from above.

The next instruction about prayer that Jesus gave His disciples dealt with *how* to pray: "And when you pray, do not use vain repetitions as the heathen *do*. For they think that they will be heard for their many words" (Matthew 6:7).

Our prayers can tend to get wordy, as if quantity meant as much as quality. It doesn't. This is not a game of Scrabble. You will not score more points by using lots of words. As we have already discussed, concentration can be hard under the best of circumstances. So the longer you ramble on, the greater the danger that your mind will wander. I have caught myself "coming to" in the middle of a prayer and wondering what I had been saying.

Short prayers are better than long ones, which can sound like the minutes of the previous meeting when we offer them to God in a distracted way. We can learn again from St. John of Kronstadt, a busy parish priest who still managed to be holy: "If you have not time to say all the prayers, it does not matter, and you will receive incomparably greater benefit from praying frequently and not hurriedly, than if you say all your prayers hurriedly, and without feeling." St. Seraphim of Sarov, one of the greatest saints in the Russian Orthodox Church, had a very short rule of prayer he gave to people he knew were too busy to spend lots of time in prayer. Firing off prayers from your spiritual machine-gun, without being able to pay attention to what you are saying, obeys the letter of the law but kills its spirit.

The Lord's Prayer is a good example of how to pray. It says just what needs to be said, and nothing more. It begins with praise and glory to the Father, gives priority to accomplishing *His* will, asks forgiveness, and petitions for our needs, all in fifty-five words. Jesus meant it to be a model. This, or any other short prayer, said slowly and with attention, is a more fruitful offering than ten pages of morning prayers squeezed into five minutes.

Speak directly and simply to God. If you are just starting a prayer life, limit yourself to no more than fifteen minutes at a time. If you are not in the habit of disciplined prayer, even that amount may be difficult for you to do. If so, at first just pray as long as you can. With practice you will discover that the time you spend in prayer increases.

A good rule to remember when praying is to KISS: Keep It Short and Simple. Do not worry in advance about what you will say—the Holy Spirit will take care of that. Do not be concerned about how to do it. Just follow the step-by-step instructions that Jesus gives in the sixth chapter of Matthew. And, if you are a beginner, do not attempt more than you can handle. Make the sign of the Cross, say the Lord's Prayer, and speak directly to God from your heart.

Chapter 3

Knowledge of the Glory

But we all, with unveiled face, behold-
ing as in a mirror the glory of the Lord,
are being transformed into the same im-
age from glory to glory.
—2 Corinthians 3:18

We pray in order to communicate with God, to learn His will for us, and to offer ourselves to Him. At first, as in any new relationship, things may feel a bit superficial. When meeting new friends, we do not immediately reveal all our family secrets. Trust must be established before open relationship begins.

But as real friendship continues, it deepens and becomes more honest. We feel comfortable telling things about ourselves to someone else because we trust him or her. As we open ourselves more to the other, we may find what the Celtic Christians called a "soul friend." A soul friend was someone you would open up to regarding your spiritual life, discussing problems, sins, delusions, or anything that could pose a problem about Christian life. Just as you might discuss yesterday's football game with friends at work, so with a soul friend you would discuss spiritual matters. A soul friend holds you accountable and keeps you honest and focused, and does not accept any nonsense.

As any relationship continues, it should grow to a deeper and more personal level than where it began. Our relationship with God should develop in the same way. At first, it can be scary to open yourself completely to anyone, let alone the Author of life! So at first we may be a bit tentative, even with God. Most of us have been let down by friends in the past, and some of us may even feel we have been let down by God. Although your brain says you can trust God, your heart wants to be sure.

Have you ever explored a cave? Beginning a prayer life is like standing at the edge of a large opening in the ground. As we look down, we can see a path spiraling away into the darkness. Our journey lies down that path into an unfamiliar place, and we cannot see very far ahead. Along the way, there will be levels where we can rest, but always we have to move further down into the depth of that mystery.

Or perhaps you prefer to climb. You start at the bottom of a mountain and carefully make your way to the top. Few climbers move in a straight line from bottom to top, because a straight line may not be the most efficient route. Although the path may continue on one level for a while, climbers will always have to move to a higher level, if they want to reach the top.

Actually, both analogies together may help us understand the life of prayer. When we start to pray, we enter into ourselves. In the cave analogy, that is the dark, downward movement to an unfamiliar place. St. Makarios points out that the mysteries of the kingdom are within us, but his was not an original idea. Jesus said, "The kingdom of God is within you" (Luke 17:21). God dwells within us, and at first, that is where we will encounter Him. Through prayer and repentance, you will discover more parts of yourself that must be offered to God, either for healing or for sanctification. Because sin takes you away from God's light, and there is much sin within all of us, your journey will take you down into some of the dark places of your soul.

There we meet what, for the world, is a paradox. The more of our sinful self we discover that needs to be purged by God's light, the more of God's light we discover already dwelling inside of us. The more dark places are disclosed, the more light shines, and we are transformed into God's image. We move "from glory to glory" (2 Corinthians 3:18). It is a bit like going with the disciples up Mt. Tabor for the Transfiguration.

The important thing to remember is that prayer implies movement—either closer toward God or further away from Him. Why would we want to move away? Well, the more you learn about God, the more you will understand that He is not "safe"—at least for the person who wants to hang onto his old way of life. God is not safe for the person who does not want to change. God is a lion, not a pussycat; and as C. S. Lewis said of the Lion Aslan, the Christ figure in *The Chronicles of Narnia*, "He's not a *tame* lion." He is a God of power and wonder, and He can effect great change in us. If we are comfortable as we are, this realization can be worrisome. You must count the cost. Prayer will cost you life as you know it.

So you may advance in awe, or run in fear. That choice God leaves to you. One thing you cannot do once you have met God in prayer is to remain where you are.

✦ Further Up and Further In ✦

In his book, *The Last Battle*, C. S. Lewis gives us a wonderful image of mankind entering heaven. Aslan the Lion keeps running ahead of the "faithful," leading them into ever-greater wonders. And all the time he keeps encouraging them, calling, "Further up and further in!" If we keep at it, our prayer will lead us to this.

As your relationship with God develops, you will discover

that you grow through various stages of maturity. Things that seemed hard at first, such as keeping to a prayer rule, will, with experience, become easier. A distraction that bothered you before will no longer do so, and a practice that may once have been helpful will cease to be so. Our experience of God grows and changes as we do.

You will find that there are different levels of prayer in which you will function. What follows is not meant to be the ultimate explanation of such things, and different spiritual writers may use different terms, but generally the experience of those who pray breaks down as follows.

✦ The First Level ✦

The most basic level of communication with God is *oral prayer*, or to put it simply, "saying your prayers" out loud. You will need a prayerbook with prayers written in it that you can use. That may seem awfully basic, but you would be surprised at the number of people who are unaware of how important these first steps are. There are many good prayerbooks in print, and you can consult your pastor regarding which one to use. At this first level of prayer, use written prayers—prayers that were originally someone else's words.

Here you may hear objections. The Society for Hanging-Loose Spirituality has many members who will tell you that reading prayers is artificial, because these words are not really your own. And at first, that may be true. But the same thing could be said about the Lord's Prayer, and I rarely hear any objections to using that! Jesus told the disciples, "Pray like this . . ." and then gave them specific words that were His, not theirs. It is through use that those words become our expression of prayer as well.

At the beginning level, using written prayers (including the

Lord's Prayer) is like having training wheels on a bicycle. When you are first learning to ride, you need something to help keep you upright until you master the technique. This is what we do when we use written prayers, and it's important for those who are beginners at prayer to understand, because there is a temptation to "reinvent the wheel." We assume either that we have to make this up as we go, or that the experience of other believers is unimportant for us. This is pride—snare number one. The life of God's Church has been enriched by many holy people before us, and it is foolish and arrogant to ignore what they say.

At the first level of prayer, it is important that we be rooted in the mind of the Church. Using prayers that have been hallowed by time and use is one of the ways we do that. Otherwise we are in danger of wandering away from sound doctrine, developing our own religion as we go. It is amazing how quickly this can happen. Nothing can color our image of God like the words that we use to communicate with Him, and we can wind up worshiping a god who is a far cry from the God we find in the Bible. Using written prayers that have been tested against the teaching of the Church can help us keep to sound doctrine so that we do not end up worshiping ourselves. Those of you who were looking for some creative effort can relax. You *will* go beyond using written prayers, but not before you are grounded in "the apostles' doctrine and fellowship" (Acts 2:42).

The first level of prayer is one of awkward discovery, like dating for the first time. There we are, praying along, when we catch a glimpse of our Beloved, walking among the valleys and skipping atop the hills. Before we know it, we have fallen for Him, and then what do we do? Probably try to think of something original to say. But, as on that first date, we will likely blurt out something embarrassingly stupid that does not express our true feelings at all. We need the experience of someone older and wiser in the ways of love—a Cyrano de Bergerac who can give us some great lines. Thus the need for the written prayers.

❧ *The Orthodox Mind-Meld* ❧

After you have disciplined yourself to saying your prayers, in God's time you will begin to experience the second level of prayer, which is called *mental prayer*. As the prayers you use become more a part of you, you become accustomed to concentrating on God, rather than on the words of prayer. Impelled by your desire, you rejoice in His presence. Your attention becomes more focused, and when that happens, the Spirit can really begin to lead you into prayer.

This is when you start speaking your own prayers in your own words, *in addition* to the written ones. There will always be a need for written prayers, but as you progress, the amount of time given to written prayers will decrease, while the amount of time spent in mental prayer will increase. It should be your goal for this to happen. No one in college should still be reading on a first-grade level, and we should not be praying that way either. This has been the experience of the saints, and with effort, it will be ours as well.

In mental prayer, we are willing ourselves to pray. We actively concentrate on what we are doing. We have to pay attention to what we say and how we say it. The Holy Spirit is active, support-ing and guiding our effort, but we must be cooperative and at-tentive. Although effective prayer may not depend entirely on our effort, our effort is still important.

For many of us, mental prayer may become the primary way in which we reach out to God. But there is a stage beyond this that we may experience as well, which is the level of *feel-ing prayer*.

❖ *The Groaning Within* ❖

St. Paul bids us to pray "without ceasing" (1 Thessalonians 5:17). When he wrote "without ceasing," he meant just that, but if you have ever tried to do it, you might be forgiven for thinking that unceasing prayer is impossible. Until we reach the level of feeling prayer, it probably is.

Feeling prayer is what Paul wrote about in Romans 8:26, which we have already quoted. The Holy Spirit moves within us, bubbling up like a spring—sometimes with good words, sometimes with groans and sighs that are intelligible only to God. It may become a continuous offering like the Jesus Prayer, or "Lord, have mercy." We cannot program this, or push a button to make it happen, because feeling prayer comes from the Spirit dwelling in us. But our spiritual effort—our praying, fasting, etc.—cleanses our soul, making it possible for the Holy Spirit to work more freely within us.

The presence of God becomes so real for us that we cannot help but pray! Your prayer will not always be verbal, and it will not be inhibited by time, space, or activity. In other words, prayer may take place *even while we are doing other things.* Our heart will reach out to God at all times!

For some, this level of prayer may be infrequent, and for others it may be constant. It should be the goal of all our striving, but it is ultimately a gift from God, and it will only happen after perseverance and hard work on our part. There is no growth without struggle, and anyone who tells you that spiritual growth happens apart from spiritual effort is off-base. Anything that can block the Spirit working in us must be rooted out, and that does not happen automatically—it comes from self-examination, repentance, and confession of our sins.

If you are sincere and disciplined in your efforts, you will make progress in prayer. But remember that your goal is union with God, not experiencing a particular kind of prayer. The Spirit leads us and knows what we need. So don't pray with checklist in hand, trying to grade your experience alongside that of St. Antony in the desert. We are all unique creatures of God, with our own personalities and needs. One person's experience will not be exactly the same as someone else's. So pray without worrying about what level you are on, and let God be in charge.

✦ *Helpful Hints* ✦

When Jesus prayed, He often went off to an isolated place where He would be undisturbed. His own discipline was the basis for His telling us to pray in secret. A quiet place is essential for recollection, which is the art of pulling yourself together so that you can concentrate on God. We cannot just turn off the world and turn on God.

Preparation is important for effective prayer. When you settle down to pray, do not begin immediately, but give yourself some time to switch gears mentally. If you had just come from work to the golf course, you would take a few practice swings before beginning the game. This is the same idea.

Silence is essential to good prayer, so be quiet for a few moments before beginning your prayers. But don't overdo it, or concentration will become a problem and you will find yourself distracted before you even start! When you are quietly settled, begin.

As you become accustomed to praying, you will want to have some time for silence between prayers. Prayer is dialogue, conversation. Give God the chance to say something if He wants to. If you approach your prayers as a set formula to be gotten through at all costs, you will program yourself for failure. Conversation means give-and-take, giving God the opportunity to say something if He wants to. One of the reasons we may never hear from God is that He can't get a word in edgewise! So space your prayers with quiet, and listen.

Whatever prayers you are using, remember to take time over the words. Say them carefully and reverently. Think about what the words mean. Allow them to sink into your soul. This is even more necessary with a familiar prayer like the Lord's Prayer. If you have too many prayers to be able to do this, then cut some out.

Scripture reading is a good springboard to prayer. Regular Bible reading provides the living witness to God that forms the context of prayer. It also establishes the sound doctrine we need in order to pray effectively. In addition, the Psalms are useful as oral prayers.

Above all, avoid the trap of assuming that praying is a substitute for worship and receiving the sacraments. The Church's worship gives a breadth of vision to our personal prayers that they would not otherwise have, keeping them from being completely centered on ourselves. St. Ambrose of Milan wrote about this: "You are told to pray especially for the people, that is, for the whole body, for all its members, the family of your mother the Church; the badge of membership is your love for each other. If you pray only for yourself, you pray for yourself alone. If each one prays for himself, he receives less from God's goodness than the one who prays on behalf of others." Being with other members of the Body of Christ in worship helps us to remember their needs as well as our own.

Whatever happens, keep at it! St. Benedict taught his monks that "prayer is work." At first things might even go well. New experiences are always exciting. But as the newness wears off, harder times will follow. The lives of the saints show us that praying will involve times of dryness, doubt, and despair. It goes with the territory. No pain, no gain. To produce fruit, you will have to work hard. Be patient and persistent. Those who endure to the end have a Kingdom to gain.

Chapter 4

Here There Be Dragons

O Lord, God of my salvation,
I have cried out day and night before You.
—Psalm 88:1

Let's look at some of the difficulties we will meet in prayer. We will learn as much from our bad experiences as from our good ones—possibly more.

One of the most frequent temptations during prayer is to wonder if anyone is really listening. "Is there anyone out there?" can easily come to mind when we pray and nothing seems to happen. It may or may not be a case of not getting what we want. It may just seem that *nothing* happens. No matter how genuine our faith, there will be times when we question whether or not God pays attention. And we will ask for things our entire lives that we will never receive. If what we have requested is not very important, our disappointment will be small. But what about those times we pray for someone to be healed, and he is not? What if we pray for someone to live, and she dies? How can our Beloved refuse us?

✦ *Praying with Confidence* ✦

The logical conclusion is that God either does not hear us or does not care. What good is our believing, if God does not respond?

33

Yet it can just as easily be asked, Will we believe in God only if
He jumps through every hoop we ask Him to? A relationship like
that is not based on faith, but on greed! We should love God
because He is God, and for no other reason. If our faith is really a
version of "The more You bless me the more I will love You,"
then we have a problem. Our faith in, and love for, God should
be based on who He is—the One who has given us life.

Yet Jesus has told us to ask for things. "Ask, and it will be
given to you" (Matthew 7:7). It is normal for children to ask for
things from their Father. And when we ask and do not receive,
we feel let down.

God always answers prayer. He may not, however, answer the
way we want Him to. If I go to the bank for a loan, and if, after
looking at my finances, the bank refuses me, I can hardly com-
plain that I received no answer. The answer was "no." That is
often the answer we get from God, but it is no less an answer just
because He said "no."

There is a dangerous trend in some modern Christian circles
that assumes all answers to real prayer will be "yes." Some teachers tell us to "expect a miracle," and if we have faith, we will receive
what we ask for. (This can do a real "number" on those who wind
up blaming their own lack of faith for a negative response.)

It is true that Jesus said if we ask anything in His name we
will receive it, but there are some important conditions. "Now
this is the confidence that we have in Him, that if we ask anything
according to His will, He hears us" (1 John 5:14, emphasis mine).

The important words here are "according to His will." It is
amazing how many people seem to miss that. We are promised
not a free run on the "goodies," but rather those things that God
wills us to have. And since God wills our salvation, the things we
ask for must be concerned with that. The verse from 1 John makes
the point that the confidence with which we make a request is

based, not on the request itself, but on the knowledge that it reflects God's will. The only time we can be certain God's answer will be "yes" is when we are absolutely certain of what His will is! That kind of arrogant certitude can be dangerous.

❧ *A Hard Lesson* ❧

Never assume that your priorities are the same as God's. "'For My thoughts *are* not your thoughts, / Nor *are* your ways My ways,' says the Lord" (Isaiah 55:8). If we project our will onto God, we are playing an ego game under the guise of piety. Only God knows the eternal consequences of saying "yes" to our prayer. And only He knows why it is often better for us *not* to receive what we ask for. It is His blessed way of helping us preserve our sanity and achieve our salvation.

Given our tendency to live for the present, this can be difficult to learn. Deferred gratification is hard to accept. (Lord grant me patience, NOW!) And there is always the danger that we might just get what we want, and regret it. During my ministry, I have had the experience many times of storming heaven with prayers, asking for the solution to a problem in a way that I was convinced was best. Unfortunately, I didn't look down the road to see the possible consequences of what I had asked for. Often the situation would work out just as I "knew" it should, only to blow up later in my face. God always responds. Be grateful for the times He has said "no."

In the Epistle of James, we find some pointed comments on the matter of asking and receiving. "You ask and do not receive, because you ask amiss, that you may spend *it* on your pleasures" (James 4:3). Much of what we ask God for is unnecessary and is based on our wants, rather than our needs. God has promised to provide *what we need*—read Matthew 6:25–34—but this tends to fall short of what we want.

Yet there are Christian teachers in our time, as there have been in others, who want us to accept that all that is necessary to receive something is that we ask for it with enough faith—regardless of how worldly those desires may be. That new Cadillac will certainly show the world how much God loves me!

This is a spirituality based on greed, and it is a good sign that our priorities are off. Instead of asking for our daily bread, we start thinking in terms of our daily croissant, concentrating on our pleasures. Christian worldliness is no more attractive than any other kind, no matter how much piety we use as cover. If you ask for material things, know that you must give an account to God of how you have used them. "No one can serve two masters; for either he will hate the one and love the other, or else he will be loyal to the one and despise the other. You cannot serve God and mammon" (Matthew 6:24). If you want material things, pray away—and be prepared to duck.

✦ *Praying with Blinders* ✦

One reason for continual prayer is that it helps us to see things from God's perspective. One of the greatest problems in the spiritual life is that our vision of the world is limited, whereas God's vision is unlimited and eternal. If we are frequent in prayer, we place everything we pray for into a different perspective—God's! God shares His life with us, and as we draw closer to Him, we can begin to see with His eyes.

Consider one practical problem that most of us face at one time or another: praying for our enemies, those who hate us. However hard this might be—and praying for those who have it in for us is never easy—we lift them up to God when we pray, and we begin to see our enemies in connection with God. Because we pray to the Father through the Son, we see our enemy through Christ's eyes, which means looking at him through Christ's loving, forgiving, compassionate gaze.

You cannot persistently look at someone with Christ's vision without coming to love him, because Jesus loves him. We tend to enjoy our resentments, so this can take a long time; however, we will eventually come to see such people, not as our enemies, but as persons who are loved, cherished, and called to salvation by our God. Our feelings about them will start to change. Nothing may happen to them, by the way—they still may have it in for us! But much will happen to us. We will not hold their sins against them, and we will cease to be resentful towards them. This is why Jesus teaches us to bless our persecutors. It is less for their sakes than for our own.

We cannot know what the future holds, either for us or for others, but God does. We must trust Him to respond on the basis of His knowledge, not our wishes.

✦ *Distractions* ✦

Distraction is what often occurs when we try to concentrate on any task. Try to take a shower, and the phone will ring. If you are trying to study, someone will turn on the television. And if you try concentrating on God, you will be bombarded with all kinds of things that have nothing to do with the task at hand. It is one of the most common problems in the spiritual life. You settle down to talk with God, and you get an instant replay of that argument you just had with your spouse. Or you start thinking about problems from work. A kaleidoscope of images will pop up to confuse and distract you. You may even have temptations that attack the senses and seek to lead you toward evil.

This will be irritating, but don't panic! One of the causes of this is the division that sin brings into our lives. Our passions always try to overrule our hearts. Mind, soul, and heart do not function as the integrated whole that God intended for them to be. St. Gregory of Sinai writes that the origin of distractions, especially of evil thoughts, is "the splitting up, through man's transgression, of his single and simple memory." Before the Fall, our attention was focused on God, where it belonged. Since sin has been let loose in our lives, there are all kinds of things that are competing for that attention.

It is possible to overcome distraction and even evil thoughts. If you are praying and find your attention diverted, gently and firmly bring your attention back to where it belongs. Looking at a cross or an icon can help focus the attention, which is why the Church surrounds us with them: turn your eyes from the person or situation that distracts you, and turn them toward something holy. All of the Fathers write about the necessity of guarding our senses, especially the eyes and ears, from sights and sounds that can tempt us. Do not become upset by the distraction, because the resulting emotion gives rise to more distraction, compounding the problem. This technique will enable us to handle most simple distractions.

✦ Looking for the Cause ✦

However, if a specific distraction is persistent, you need to look for its cause, then seek to overcome it. For example, how is your health? Poor physical conditioning can lead to poor spiritual conditioning. We need to exercise, eat properly, and get enough rest. This may sound mundane, but it is very important. It is hard to concentrate on God at nine A.M. if we were up watching television until four A.M.! Fatigue dulls our ability to concentrate, and a little common sense can do wonders for our prayer life.

The next question we should ask ourselves is, Are we really ready to pray? Are we following the basic instructions? Have we gone into our room and shut the door—either actually or figuratively? Have we tried to shut out the world so we can concentrate on heaven? If we do not settle down to a quiet atmosphere for prayer, we will probably be distracted by something. So unplug the phone—that way it cannot ring. If possible, finish any pressing tasks before prayer, so that they will not be on your mind. If you cannot postpone the laundry without worrying about it, do that first.

No prayer life will be fruitful unless you exercise self-discipline. If you have problems staying with *any* task long enough to finish it, you can expect that pattern to continue in prayer. All of life must be disciplined. Fasting, study, and work habits need to become consistent and regular. Do not expect bad habits to disappear just because you drop to your knees. Prayer can help discipline our lives, but bad habits can make praying more difficult.

There are times when distraction comes from too much discipline. Enthusiastic beginners often try to do too much. When you are not used to praying regularly, a lengthy routine becomes burdensome and makes you an easy target for distraction. It is possible to become so wrapped up in concerns about technique, method, and "getting it right" that you become fearful of making mistakes. So you freeze up and cannot pray. Then your discipline becomes a distraction, and you need to reexamine, with proper guidance, what you are doing.

Evil thoughts, as opposed to minor disturbances, can, and will, be a problem. When I say evil thoughts, I refer to those intrusive images that would lead us to sin if we let them. St. Isaac the Syrian points out that these may come from different sources: the natural desires of our own bodies; the remembrance of things we have experienced or seen; some mental or spiritual aberration of our own; or the assaults of demons.

Certainly the devil is behind much of this. He does not want us to pray. His aim is to lead us to sin in either thought or deed, and he will use anything to tempt us, even good things. When Satan confronted Jesus, he tempted the Lord by suggesting things that might make Jesus' job easier—in other words, the devil taunted Jesus to prove He was the Messiah by doing signs and wonders. Certainly a thought about serving God can be twisted by Satan into a worry about being prideful. He might whisper, "All you really want is for people to notice you," which leads to anxiety, which generally leads to inaction. Score one for the visiting team.

We can combat this by taking an honest look at how few workers in the vineyard there really are, how God calls us all to service, and how rarely people notice us anyway: in other words, do a reality check. For this level of temptation, this is normally all we need to do.

More fervent attacks need a stronger counterattack. The temptations may be sexual in nature, or rooted in resentment and anger. To these, most of us respond all too readily. Jesus reminds us, "For out of the heart proceed evil thoughts, murders, adulteries, fornications, thefts, false witness, blasphemies" (Matthew 15:19). We carry all too many of these evil thoughts around in our hearts: buttons ready to be pushed when we start to move closer to God. When our buttons are pushed, we are responding to what the holy fathers and mothers call the *passions*.

St. Diadochos of Photiki once wrote that the heart is capable of producing both good and evil thoughts. But the evil thoughts are not produced naturally—they come from the memory of evil. Sin repeated becomes a habit, and habits make for strong memories. If, for example, someone has committed adultery, he may stop the act, but the remembrance of it may linger. Unless he truly repents and overcomes the remembrance as a delightful fantasy, he is going to have problems with distraction. Spiritual growth is not just a question of removing the negative thoughts and acts from our lives, but of replacing the negative with something positive. In this case, it could mean specifically praying for the salvation of the person that one sinned with.

It is important to see just how serious this can be. A thought planted or used by the devil will not just go away. It will remain until we give in to it or get rid of it. This is part of spiritual warfare, with emphasis on warfare! Prayer is not for the timid, and if you really want to pray, you are going to have a real struggle.

There are several ways to overcome evil thoughts. First, you must be *watchful* and *attentive*. We must be on guard all the time. "Be sober, be vigilant; because your adversary the devil walks about like a roaring lion, seeking whom he may devour. Resist him, steadfast in the faith, knowing that the same sufferings are experienced by your brotherhood in the world" (1 Peter 5:8, 9). The experience of all the saints is that Satan will try to catch you when you are unwary. Go into the spiritual life with your eyes open, knowing full well that there will be spiritual struggle. If you think you will be able to pray and not have to deal with what everyone else has had to combat, you have been fooled.

There is a word that you will encounter if you do any reading in Orthodox spiritual literature. That word is *hesychia*, which literally means "to be still" or silent. *Hesychasm* is a hallmark of the Orthodox approach to spirituality. It refers to cutting off outer distractions to prayer by withdrawing from outward stimulations into the "room" of one's heart, as Jesus teaches. This concept is important for beginners to learn, although it is at first difficult to achieve. Hence the suggestions about unplugging the phone, etc.

But keeping watch over our souls involves more than just finding a quiet place to pray: it incorporates a kind of inward hesychia that strives to cut off even those inner stimulations that can distract us at prayer. Only in this way can you begin to know your own heart as God already knows it. The anger, resentment,

and sexual temptations that disrupt the life of prayer can be overcome by this kind of watchfulness, because we see them for what
they are—*not* overwhelming urges, but stimulations that do not
have to lead to action.

So dealing with distractions means we must avoid their causes,
to prevent the distraction from even arising. Most of us know
what our weak points are, but we often don't take sensible pre-
cautions to avoid falling because of them. And sometimes we go
out of our way to find situations in which failure is almost assured. If you are a recovering alcoholic, applying for a job in a
liquor store is not the smartest thing you could do. If sexual images are a problem for you, best you should cancel the subscrip-
tion to *Playboy*. Avoiding temptation is often much easier than
overcoming it *after* it appears, especially if you have opened the
door and invited it in.

Other elements of the spiritual life, such as fasting and
almsgiving, are some of the best tools used to overcome distracting thoughts. If our prayer is distracted, we may have to
pray more fervently in order to chase the thoughts off, but in
addition we must be doing the other things necessary to discipline our lives.

On the assumption that the best defense is often a strong
offense, a good way to deal with distractions is to cut them off, or
scorn them. Obviously it would be best not to allow distracting
thoughts into our heart at all, but when they do come in, tell
these thoughts to take a long walk off a short pier—"Away with
you, Satan!" (Matthew 4:10). Otherwise you run the risk of actually getting into some sort of inner debate with the distraction,
rather than showing it the door.

Begin a counterattack as soon as the distraction begins. Prayer,
preferably prayer in which the name of Jesus is used, is usually
the most effective weapon, because the name of Jesus has great

power over evil, especially the demons. Praying watchfully, invoking the name of Jesus, can clear the mind of distracting images and evil thoughts. And always pray in hope! Putting your trust in God, even when it seems useless or you don't feel like it, will be a distraction to Satan—he really hates it when we live in trust.

We are intelligent creatures with minds, so thoughts are going to arise in them. We cannot simply not think. Someone once said to one of the Desert Fathers, "Abba, I have many thoughts and they put me in danger." The old man led him out and said to him, "Expand your chest and do not breathe in." To the man's answer that he could not do it, Abba Poemen replied, "If you cannot do that, no more can you prevent thoughts from arising, but you can resist them." So can we.

❧ A Memo from the Boss ❧

Just so you don't think this is going to be too easy, I must tell you that there may be godly distractions as well. Determining what kind of distraction you are facing will require some discernment, and—yes, you guessed it—prayer.

If a particular distraction or thought is persistent, but does not seem to lead you toward sin, it is possible that God is trying to tell you something. Have you ever had a conversation with someone you feared would raise an uncomfortable issue? Perhaps there is an overdue loan or a commitment unfulfilled. We rattle on because any stop in the flow of our words might give the opportunity for the other person to raise the very subject we wish to avoid.

You may want to serve God, but be nervous about what He might actually ask you to do. So when you talk to God, you keep the words flowing, informing Him about things He already knows, in an effort to prevent Him from facing you with something you want to avoid. You might be facing a responsibility you don't want to accept. If I had a church near the beach in Hawaii, God's call to minister in Wisconsin might be the last thing I'd want to hear.

There could be a problem in our life that needs our attention. We might have bills to pay, but in exercising good American consumer stewardship, we have already spent the money! God may call us to responsibility, but we pray away, hoping that if we don't give Him the chance, the subject need not come up.

God won't force us to respond, but He will keep bringing our attention back to the one issue we want to dodge, until we either acknowledge it or give up praying. We will experience His attention-getting as a distraction in prayer—be grateful it is not lightning! No one likes having his agenda rearranged, but God is nothing if not persistent. It would be better to open yourself up to whatever it is God wants to confront you with, and deal with it. You cannot pray effectively if you are resisting God.

It is possible that a distraction may originate in us, but God will use it to make us face up to something. If, for example, our prayer is disrupted by hostile thoughts about someone, it's possible the distraction may not be driven by the evil one at all. The problem could be our own anger or resentment. So we don't just just cut off this kind of thought—which would be ducking the issue—but accept the need to deal with the problem.

I once felt betrayed by someone with whom I had spoken in confidence. Having heard through the Orthodox jungle telegraph that the facts of my conversation had become known, I was convinced that my "friend" had blabbed. I dealt with the problem in the age-old way that Christians usually deal with such things—I ignored it. I told myself—holy person that I am—that I would forgive that person, and put it behind me. But my prayer life went down the proverbial tube. Every time I tried to pray, I thought of this person. I am not well disciplined at the best of times, but now, whenever I tried to pray, it was a flop. Being stubborn by nature, I fought against the obvious for some time. I really had *not* dealt with this situation the way a Christian should. My feelings of anger and betrayal kept dogging me. Whenever I tried to pray, read Scripture, or even prepare sermons, the problem was there. God did not cause the problem, but I know that He used it to make me deal with it.

Finally I bowed to the inevitable, followed Jesus' advice (Matthew 18:15ff), and told my friend that I felt he had betrayed me. It is amazing how quickly my anger dissipated as I spoke from my heart about what had been bothering me. This was quickly replaced by a feeling of complete stupidity when my friend pointed out that he had not been the one to break my confidence—something I discovered for myself several days later. He has been very good about it; he never mentions it above three or four times a year. And since I now knew who had been involved, I moved quickly to remove any distraction by dealing with the correct person.

The point is that I resolved the distraction and removed a burden. When problems like this appear, we need to deal with the person or situation as soon as we can, or we will make no progress in prayer.

❧ Bricks Without Straw ❦

It is possible that your distractions may arise from the fact that there is not much to hold your attention, because your prayers are boring. Without something to hold our interest, our attention will wander. As a fire needs fuel to burn, so our prayers need substantial fuel to keep them going, because good intentions are not enough. That fuel should be our ever-growing knowledge and love of God.

Our knowledge of God grows through relationship and study—the two go hand in hand. When your relationship with a person grows, it is because you learn more about him, which keeps you interested in him (or her). If you learned everything there was to know about someone, if you could predict how he or she would respond to every kind of circumstance, the relationship would get dull very quickly. Your knowledge and love of God grows through prayer, study, and experience, as you seek to do His will and draw close to Him.

We must immerse ourselves in God's Word, the Holy Scriptures. "When all else fails, read the instructions." The Bible contains God's instructions for living, including, as we have seen, how to pray. Scripture provides a springboard for prayer because it brings us into contact with God as He has revealed Himself to us throughout history. The Scriptures are a trustworthy record of God's faithfulness and love. When we become tired of spiritual effort, we can turn to the Bible and see how He has always responded to mankind's needs!

The further into Scripture you go, the more you learn. God is beyond your ability to comprehend completely, but the more you know of Him, the more you will know Him, so that you "may be able to comprehend with all the saints what *is* the width and length and depth and height—to know the love of Christ which passes knowledge; that you may be filled with all the fullness of God" (Ephesians 3:18, 19).

In addition to the Bible, we need to read about the lives of the saints, and what they have written about God and their lives in Him. The saints of the Church were spiritual warriors; their struggles were like ours, so we can learn from them that what is happening to us is not unique. "No temptation has overtaken you except such as is common to man" (1 Corinthians 10:13). Through the writings of or about the saints, you can see real people going from glory to glory. This is not only an encouragement, it removes a lot of our excuses as well. The saints are proof that if we want to follow God, we can!

Take advantage of every good Bible study, every catechism class, every opportunity for learning available. Ask your pastor to recommend books that contain solid teaching. Learn as much as you can, for increasing your knowledge of God will fuel your effort to seek Him in prayer.

Chapter 5

Trench Warfare

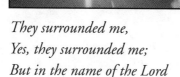

They surrounded me,
Yes, they surrounded me;
But in the name of the Lord
I will destroy them.
—Psalm 118:11

Distractions and intrusive thoughts can be a problem in the life of prayer, but there are other spiritual dangers that may have to be fought on a deeper level. The commonly used term "spiritual warfare" is not too strong an expression to describe the sort of hand-to-hand combat into which we might be drawn.

Satan does not want you to progress in prayer. As you grow closer to God, he will seek to divert you. So remember the biblical warning to be vigilant! You should not, however, allow the devil to become an excuse, either. The idea of facing a demonic attack is all too attractive to some Christians, who never want to deal with their own imperfection. Blaming anyone, including the inhabitants of the infernal regions, is better than facing themselves.

So, if you are struggling in your prayer, don't jump to the conclusion that you are under attack by outside forces. Always check first for the simplest solution to any problem you encounter. If what disturbs you cannot be put down to some practical difficulty, like trying to pray with the television on, or if it does not respond to the methods offered for dealing with intrusive thoughts, then, and only then, should you consider that something more sinister might be involved.

There is no point in giving the devil *more* than his due. Assuming that *our* problems should be laid at his door can be prideful, for there is something seductive in the notion that we are so holy that it takes the enemy's best shots to knock us off track.

It is possible that advancing in your prayer life may result in Satan trying to divert you. If he can do so without your knowing it, so much the better for him. After all, he doesn't want us to be on our guard. If we are wise to him, however, we may still overcome him.

How bad can it get? Bad, very bad, but most of us won't have to worry about the really nasty stuff. The lives of the saints can give us a glimpse of what *could* happen to someone who seeks to be holy.

St. Athanasius wrote the *Life of Antony*, a vivid account of the trials of the holy monk who is regarded as the father of monasticism. St. Antony had given all he had to the poor and gone out into the silence of the Egyptian desert to concentrate on prayer and discipline. At first, the devil simply tried to disrupt his concentration with noise at night and with disturbing thoughts during the day. (Since this was before cable, Antony could be fairly certain that he hadn't left the TV on, and there was no telephone to ring.) The devil even assumed the disguise of an attractive woman in order to tempt the monk, but Antony wouldn't bite. When he failed to get a response, Satan reverted to his actual demonic form, hoping to inspire fear in Antony.

Much to the devil's annoyance, nothing worked with this

guy. "When the enemy could stand it no longer—for he was apprehensive that Antony might before long fill the desert with discipline—approaching one night with a multitude of demons, he whipped him with such force that he lay on the earth, speechless from tortures." Still, Antony hung in there.

The next night was worse. Ever thought you had a date from hell? Well, Antony really did. "The demons, as if breaking through the building's four walls, and seeming to enter through them, were changed into the forms of beasts and reptiles. The place was immediately filled with the appearances of lions, bears, leopards, bulls, and serpents, asps, scorpions, and wolves. . . . Struck and wounded by them, Antony's body was subject to more pain."

Nasty, wasn't it! But before you head for the nearest exit, relax! Most of us are nowhere *near* the holiness of an Antony; Satan reserves this kind of direct assault for those he cannot overcome any other way. Humbling as it may be to admit, we are probably not among these people. But what happened to Antony, and other saints, serves to bring up an important point: There is a direct connection between your closeness to God and the problems you will face. Holiness does not become easier as you go, it becomes harder to attain. As you become more mature—more practiced at what you do—the more necessary it will be for Satan to send in the heavy artillery. You have been warned.

If you do face incoming attacks from the other side, there are some good defensive weapons at hand. Pray, fast, and continue on with your job, telling the devil to go to—well, to get lost. Satan cannot stand being ignored, so be prepared for his tantrum. The fact is, though, he has no real power over you, unless you give it to him by caving in to fear. "Therefore submit to God. Resist the devil and he will flee from you" (James 4:7). Like most bullies, Satan runs when you stand up to him.

✦ *Wandering in the Desert* ✦

A more common problem is the spiritual dryness that will eventually trip up everyone. There will be times when you try to pray and you cannot. You don't seem to be doing anything wrong, but the words will not come. Everyone—even the saints—hits the wall at one time or another, but that knowledge doesn't give much comfort when you are the one who feels he is wandering in the desert. And when you are lost in the desert, the sand just seems to go on forever.

The greatest danger here is that the resulting frustration can lead to despair, and to surrender. The problem is not so much intellectual as emotional—it hits you right in your gut. All your fervor and enthusiasm seem to vanish. The desire for your Beloved is not there, and you wonder if you were ever really in love with God at all.

Then doubt sets in. You think that maybe God doesn't really care. Your efforts seem useless, and anything that was good about your prayer life is quickly forgotten. A downward spiral begins that leads to doubting your faith in general, as well as specific beliefs. (Questioning the reality of the presence of Jesus in the Eucharist seems to be a hallmark of this latter condition; perhaps the sense of His presence is what we are missing.) "I opened for my beloved, / But my beloved had turned away *and* was gone" (Song of Solomon 5:6). We feel abandoned.

When dealing with any spiritual problem, we should always return to the basics. First, we have to remember that God is always present, whether it seems so to us or not. His existence does not depend on how we are feeling about Him at any given time. "Where can I go from Your Spirit? / Or where can I flee from Your presence? / If I ascend into heaven, You *are* there; / If I make my bed in hell, behold, You *are there*" (Psalm 139:7, 8). Continue to act in the knowledge (not the feeling) that God *is* there.

Make the sign of the cross and call on the name of Jesus. If mental or feeling prayer is impossible, return to the basic foundation of oral prayer. This is when a prayerbook can be most helpful, because you can offer the written prayers instead of trying to force out your own words. Say the Lord's Prayer slowly, with reflection. The words of others who have prayed effectively are no small offering—especially when you have nothing else to offer.

Spiritual reading can be used to combat dryness—particularly something that has been meaningful in the past, and may get the juices flowing again. Reading is not meant to take the place of praying, but it can provide a jumpstart. Read slowly, without intending to cover lots of material (this is not a good time to start *War and Peace*). Open yourself to the ideas, and stop occasionally to see if prayer does come. If not, continue reading.

Remember that your purpose is prayer, not reading. Do not become so caught up in the material that you forget what you are supposed to be doing. Limit your reading time to the amount that you would have spent in prayer. It is still important to keep to your discipline about time and place, even if nothing seems to happen. Once your basic rhythm is lost, it will be that much harder to get on track again. At least reading uses your time well.

Do not play around with mechanics: "Well, if standing doesn't work, I'll try kneeling; if this set of prayers does nothing for me, I'll use another." Doing this disrupts your basic rhythm, and your discipline will start to unravel. Soon, you will get totally caught up in your search for something different, convinced that if you can just find the right combination of words, posture, and mental attitude, everything will return to normal. It won't.

If you concentrate too much on what is happening to you, your problem ceases to be one of prayer, and becomes one of self-centeredness. This kind of self-centeredness does not feed your pride as much as your despair. You start to worry about "poor me," with a capital ME. That, in turn, can lead to depression and getting down on ourselves, which only makes our recovery harder. We become so discouraged that we give up.

Taking a break from prayer doesn't work either. It just makes us lazy and self-indulgent. One of the purposes of spiritual effort is to glorify God as best we can. Even when functioning imperfectly, we can still make the best offering possible under the circumstances: "A mercy of peace, a sacrifice of praise." But we must have the will to offer.

Emotions are powerful, and we have seen how they can be fertile ground for distraction. Depression, anger, and hurt make prayer more difficult. But the basis of our prayer effort must be in our will, not our feelings. If we do good things only when we feel like it, we will rarely accomplish anything important. We must make a conscious decision to pray—when things are going well, *and* when they are not. In a fallen world, nothing godly is automatic. You cannot allow your emotions to be an excuse for giving up. Your *intention* to be with God can still be present even when there are no feelings of devotion. That may not sound like much to us, but God will accept it with joy, because it shows that we are serious, and He will respond to our intent. It becomes a *sacrifice* of praise.

Teresa of Avila was a Spanish mystic—the veteran of many spiritual battles. She looked on periods of dryness as gifts from God, which may help us understand them better. She, and other mystical writers, believed that at the start of our spiritual effort, the reward may be easy because God knows how quickly we become discouraged. So He is merciful, and the beginning of our prayer life may be quite enjoyable.

But after our habits have been established, God sometimes withdraws the spiritual "goodies." Just as Jesus was loath to perform miracles on demand (because He wanted faith to be rooted in truth rather than drama), God wants us to love Him for what He is, not for what He does.

This kind of learning is part of growing up. If our love for someone is real, we move from infatuation to commitment. In prayer, we must go beyond playing at devotions and get down to real work. What may seem like a spiritual disaster to us may just be God showing us that we no longer need the training wheels.

The purpose behind God's testing of our resolve is to see how deep our commitment really is, and how long we are willing to carry on. A necessary part of any learning process is going beyond where you are now. This can sometimes be extremely frustrating and very painful. Learning involves change, and change is seldom comfortable. And the ultimate lesson has to do with obedience, which is so important that even Jesus had to learn it. "Though He was a Son, *yet* He learned obedience by the things which He suffered. And having been perfected, He became the author of eternal salvation to all who obey Him" (Hebrews 5:8, 9). No pain, no gain. We are strengthened by our sufferings.

And suffering will be a part of the process. Spiritual struggle shapes and molds us into God's likeness. You must learn to trust God with a genuine faith that can survive testing, and no faith is genuine until it is tested. God is in the desert, calling you through it. You must continue on, even if you feel as if you are staggering over the sand like one of those characters in an old Foreign Legion movie. "I press toward the goal for the prize of the upward call of God in Christ Jesus" (Philippians 3:14).

Our first experience with spiritual dryness may be intense, but of short duration. Experience shows that as we grow, the periods of dryness become longer, but less acute—the sharp pain gives way to a dull, lingering ache. This is another sign of growth. You are always being called beyond where you are. There will be lots of ups and downs, but as you mature, your response will become more stable. You will get a better handle on things. Temptation will come, but the means to overcome it will be at hand.

❧ *Too Uptight* ❧

There is something that in the long run can be more dangerous than dryness: a self-critical condition called *scrupulosity*. Scrupulosity is the state of being constantly oppressed by exaggerated trifles—of making mountains out of molehills. The scrupulous person is always worried about something—making mistakes, despairing over miserable efforts, convinced that Murphy's Law will prevail. What is worse, people like this are usually pestering someone else with their concerns.

Scrupulosity can be a greater danger than dryness, because when it takes hold on a soul, paralysis sets in. We have a real case of the spiritual jitters, which makes us afraid to take any action for fear it will be wrong. Any attempt to reach God becomes a nightmare of insecurity. Tight-lipped seriousness becomes the order of the day, and there is no joy. We become so concerned about doing it right that the mechanics of prayer become more important than communicating with God.

Scrupulosity quenches the Spirit. We should approach the work of prayer with a serious spirit, certainly, but with joy and freedom as well. After all, we are able to speak with our Father and Creator in an intimate way. We will not glorify God by being gloomy, frustrated, and nervous. So, while we should never be careless, we can be quietly confident that God will bless a sincere effort.

A really good tennis player would not be one who rigidly maintained his position on the court, eyes fixed straight ahead, his racquet held tensely in front of him. He would be unable to respond flexibly to where his opponent hit the ball. A good player is relaxed but watchful, capable of responding to a variety of circumstances. The Bible says to be sober and vigilant, not para-noid and fearful.

The tense soul becomes so obsessed with dangers and problems that it loses all sense of perspective. The smallest difficulty becomes an occasion for panic. Granted, seeking God entails risk, but we need to trust in the Holy Spirit. We are not in this alone, and we cannot keep our spiritual eyes on God if we are always ducking.

In the Parable of the Talents, Jesus tells the story of a servant so afraid of making a mistake that he loses everything through excessive caution. When the servant explains to his master that he was afraid of doing anything with the money his master had left with him, for fear he would lose it, the master responds in words that anyone afraid to act should hear. "Therefore take the talent from him, and give *it* to him who has ten talents. For to everyone who has, more will be given, and he will have abundance; but from him who does not have, even what he has will be taken away" (Matthew 25:28, 29).

The point of the story is that we can lose the life God offers to us by refusing to live it! There is nothing automatic about our salvation. We must actively work on it daily. This does not take anything away from the fact that Christ has won salvation for us, but we must constantly seek to live the life of salvation in Him. Otherwise we may, in fact, lose the Kingdom!

❖ *Spiritual Delusion* ❖

I have mentioned several times that the spiritual life, and prayer particularly, can be dangerous. Some of these dangers come from the mistakes that we make and do not correct. Some may come from evil thoughts or temptations that originate from another source. But some will be the result of a deliberate attempt by Satan to confuse and mislead us.

We have seen a few of the assaults that St. Antony had to endure, including a confrontation with the devil himself. While such a confrontation is possible for those of you who are working at prayer, your confuser-in-residence is more likely to be a lower-level imp or apprentice demon. In this scenario, instead of being tempted by thoughts that are insinuated into your heart, you might have direct contact with a being who seeks to distract you.

Both angels and demons are incorporeal, which is a fancy word that means "having no body"—at least not in the sense that we have bodies. Both angels and demons (who are fallen angels) have material substance, or they could not exist. Only God is pure spirit. But they are not flesh-and-blood beings as we are. Angels act as messengers and protectors. Demons may act as messengers as well, but the message will not be designed to help, and our protection definitely will not be their concern.

It is possible that if you persevere in the life of prayer, you may have a vision of someone appearing to you, and perhaps speaking to you. If this is a genuine appearance, and not just the result of too much pepperoni pizza, then you face a problem of discerning whom this being represents—God or Satan. Can you trust what it says?

St. Gregory of Sinai wrote:

By no means accept it if you see anything sensuously or with the mind, inside or outside of you, whether it be an image of Christ or an angel or some saint, or if a light should be fancied or depicted by the imagination in the mind. For by nature it is characteristic of the mind itself to indulge in fantasies, and it easily forms the image it desires; this is usual in those who do not pay strict attention to themselves, and by this they do harm to themselves.

Assuming that what you see is real, the first thing you must determine is whether this is an angel or a demon. It would help things considerably if the field operatives of the Infernal Office would wear some sort of uniform—perhaps a red jumpsuit with H.E.L.L. spelled out on the back in large yellow letters. Unfortunately they have more sense than that. The devil himself, as Scripture reminds us, appears as an angel of light (which is what he originally was). And he knows that no sensible person will respond to anyone who looks, speaks, and smells like a demon. Its actual appearance, therefore, would be that of an angel or saint. If you allow yourself to be confused into believing that the apparition comes from God, you could wind up in some deep . . . well, molasses.

Reading the lives of the saints will be instructive. You already have seen what Antony faced, but many other holy people, down through the years, have experienced similar things. St. John Cassian, who was pivotal in establishing Orthodox monasticism in the West, recounts the story of a monk named Hero. Hero accepted the appearance of a demon as that of an angel and began to follow the demon's advice. First, the demon praised Hero's spirituality and told him how pleased God was with him. That wasn't too hard for Hero to take, and he fell for it—hook, line, and sinker. Next, having taken the monk in, the demon told Hero that God was so pleased with him that no physical harm could come to him. To prove it, the demon persuaded Hero to throw himself down a well, which had an unfortunate effect on Hero's physical well-being: he died. The real tragedy here was that Hero had become so fixated in delusion that he would not repent, even as he lay dying. He remained convinced of what he had been told by the demon.

Nothing that comes from God will scare us. It may inspire awe or a sense of being unworthy, or we may have normal human anxiety about being able to do what He calls us to do, but it will never scare us. That should be your first test: If the being that appears to you brings you fear, then it is not from God.

Secondly, test what is told you by what you already know and have experienced. If what you are told is at odds with the teaching of the Church, or with biblical morality, or even with common sense, don't pay any attention to it. Really now, does it seem sensible to you that God would single *you* out of all the faithful, tell you that you are wonderful, and suggest that you prove your worthiness by jumping off a cliff?!

Another response you can use to test an apparition is the "good defense-strong offense" strategy we used against evil thoughts. Step up to the plate and take a swing at it. In his *Life of St. Antony*, St. Ignatius Brianchaninov suggests:

> When any kind of vision presents itself, do not become frightened, but no matter what kind of vision it is, manfully ask it first of all: "Who are you, and where do you come from?" If it is a manifestation of the saints, they will calm you and will turn your fear into joy. But if it is a demonic apparition, when it encounters firmness in your soul it will immediately waver, because the question serves as a sign of a brave soul.

If the demons are capable of deceiving even the very holy, you and I need to be careful. We need to make certain that we do not set ourselves up for an attack. Asking for a vision or a sign from God may get a response, but not from the One we hope to hear from. (In my case, almost every time I have asked God to show me a sign, it has said EXXON.) There are no shortcuts in the spiritual life, and lusting after holy things—asking more from God than we either deserve or can handle—is asking for trouble.

St. Ignatius also writes, "The only correct entrance into the world of spirits is the doctrine and practice of Christian struggle. The only correct entrance into the sensuous perception of spirits is Christian advancement and perfection." When God knows we can handle such an experience, and it is time for us to have it, we will. Not before.

❖ *A Native Guide* ❖

I am a devotee of old, preferably bad, Hollywood movies. In every African safari picture that I have ever seen, the first rule is to find a native guide who can help get you through the land of the dreaded Wanatatube tribe. The guide knows the territory, and his job is to get people through the jungle safely. He can pull this off because he knows where the danger is.

A guide is one resource you should always have on your spiritual journey. You have already seen some of the dangers that can trap you. You are going to need help.

If you developed a problem with your golf swing, you would seek advice from someone who plays the game well. If your problem is with prayer, you will need advice from someone who plays the game well—someone who is experienced in Christian devotion. Two heads are better than one when you are struggling with your prayer life, and you will need the loving support of others. If nothing else, you will learn that what has happened to you is not unique—others have faced these same problems and overcome them.

You need to seek the guidance of a good spiritual director—someone who can help you sort out your difficulties and find your way. It is very easy to become so wrapped up in your struggle that you lose sight of the goal. When you are up to your hips in alligators, it is hard to remember that your original purpose was to drain the swamp. An objective view from someone who is not involved in your situation can be very helpful. By seeking competent advice, trusting in God, and continuing your effort, you can advance in prayer.

A good spiritual director may be either male or female, clergy or laity. Not everyone is good at spiritual direction, but there are competent and holy people around. Orthodox Tradition definitely sees guidance from others who are experienced in spiritual matters as a necessity. The Holy Fathers say that the person who tries to direct himself is a fool. In most cases your spiritual director will be your pastor, but if you have someone else as your spiritual father or mother, your pastor should know about it. Your spiritual director should be consulted on a regular basis, and once established, the relationship should continue unless there is a good reason to end it. Nothing is more pathetic than the soul who keeps shopping around until he finds someone who will tell him what he wants to hear.

In the Orthodox tradition we recognize the existence of a guide who is beyond the competence of a spiritual director. These persons are known as spiritual elders. Eldership is recognized in those who have been given charismatic gifts to see into our hearts and help heal what is there. These people tend to be few and far between, although there may be more out there than we realize. If it is your good fortune to encounter such a person, place yourself under his or her care and *stay there*! The Church has never lacked holy people who can show us the way to the Kingdom. Whether it is a competent confessor, director, or elder, there *are* those who can be of great help. Prayer is too important to be a "do-it-yourself" job.

Nothing worthwhile comes easily, and prayer is no exception. There will be struggles, but the reward is great. If you are in trouble, do not be embarrassed about seeking help. Cry out to God for aid. If we are faithful, He will respond, as He did to St. Antony:

Aware of assistance, and both breathing more easily and relieved from the sufferings, Antony entreated the vision that appeared, saying, "Where were you? Why didn't you appear in the beginning, so that you could stop my distresses?" And a voice came to him: "I was here, Antony, but I waited to watch your struggle. And now, since you persevered and were not defeated, I will be your helper forever." (St. Athanasius, *The Life of Antony*)

Chapter 6

Honesty

Give ear to my words, O Lord.
—Psalm 5:1

And now a few words about honest prayer. That may sound silly to you, but why pray at all, if we are not going to be honest when we do so? We may not set out to be deceitful in our prayers; in fact, most of us would probably resent the suggestion that we were not honest when we prayed. But human nature being what it is, dishonest prayer is a reality.

We are all sinners trying to overcome our imperfections. This is what Christian life is all about. The hard truth is that we fall far short of where we should be. "If we say we have no sin, we deceive ourselves, and the truth is not in us" (1 John 1:8). Part of our sinfulness is often that we refuse to admit to our sins, hiding behind a wall of defenses and excuse-making—and this behavior has consequences for our prayers.

It is human nature to want to think the best of oneself. Christians are not immune to that. We desire to put the best face on our actions, to ourselves and to others. We want others, including God, to think well of us. We acknowledge that we fall short of what we should be, but pride leads us to substitute our version of events for reality. The result is that even when we admit to being sinners, we may not admit that we are quite as bad as we really are.

Think for a moment. In childhood, how many times did your parents catch you in the act of doing wrong? And how many times, despite irrefutable evidence, did you try to talk your way out of trouble? Common sense would say to admit your actions, take your punishment, and get it over with. But survival sense says, "Lie!" For most children, stretching the truth seems justifiable if by doing so they can avoid parental wrath—it's in the Child's Survival Handbook.

As adults, we do the same thing with God. The denial patterns are as old as creation. In Genesis you can read Adam's reaction when he was caught with his hand in the proverbial cookie jar.

> Then the Lord God called to Adam and said to him, "Where *are* you?" So he said, "I heard Your voice in the garden, and I was afraid because I was naked; and I hid myself." And He said, "Who told you that you *were* naked? Have you eaten from the tree of which I commanded you that you should not eat?" Then the man said, "The woman whom You gave *to be* with me, she gave me of the tree, and I ate." (Genesis 3:9–12)

Behold, the First Excuse. Adam blames his wife, because she gave him the apple to eat in the first place. Rather than admit his wrongdoing and ask forgiveness, Adam looked for a "blame object." The designated blame object, however, was capable of some fancy footwork of her own! "And the Lord God said to the woman, 'What *is* this you have done?' The woman said, 'The serpent deceived me, and I ate'" (Genesis 3:13). The poor snake had nobody to blame. And we wonder where our children get it from!

Adam and Eve were willing to do anything—including blame-shifting—rather than admit they were responsible. Note that they did not start out to be dishonest with God. They just tried to ignore Him. Whenever *we* do that, God finds us, and then we start justifying ourselves!

I am not suggesting that from the start we intend to deceive God in our prayer. We just get nervous and allow ourselves to be taken in by the image we try to project to others—we believe our own press releases. "For now we see in a mirror, dimly" (1 Corinthians 13:12). The dimness may result from the false image of ourselves behind which we try to hide our sins.

❧ *The Need for Conversion* ❦

Many Orthodox react adversely to the word "conversion." "That's emotionalism," they respond. It is true that the word "conversion" can carry with it the negative baggage of manipulative media evangelism. Unfortunately, this baggage hides the necessity of a personal response to a personal God.

We should be careful. As many Christians have experienced it, conversion is long on emotion and short on doctrine. "Accepting Jesus" can become a shortcut past solid teaching and careful nurturing. At its worst, conversion can play with someone's emotions at a time when those emotions really need careful rebuilding.

After we have recognized the dangers, however, the fact remains that we must be converted in our relationship with God; something must change within us for spiritual growth to occur. When Jesus encountered the adulterous woman, He did not send her off with a cheery suggestion to have a nice day. He said, "Go and sin no more" (John 8:11). That meant she had to change the way she was living. Then the Lord said to those around Him, "I am the light of the world. He who follows Me shall not walk in darkness, but have the light of life" (John 8:12). Like the adulterous woman, we must stop walking in darkness—leading lives of sin—and start walking in the light! This is conversion.

St. Paul describes the process this way: "Put off, concerning your former conduct, the old man which grows corrupt according to the deceitful lusts, and be renewed in the spirit of your mind, and . . . put on the new man which was created according to God, in true righteousness and holiness" (Ephesians 4:22–24). If we follow Christ, we must become different people, taking off our old conduct and putting on the new.

In other words, if you are doing something wrong, stop it! Unless you do, you cannot enter the Kingdom of God. You must be converted. "Assuredly, I say to you, unless you are converted and become as little children, you will by no means enter the kingdom of heaven" (Matthew 18:3).

As Paul points out, there is something more involved than just cleaning up your act, as important as that is. Your mind must be renewed. Your entire vision of life must change. Action, thought, and feeling are all involved in being converted. Only then can you become whole, and becoming whole is what conversion is all about. Being converted and renewed means turning away from living for yourself and turning toward living for God. The Greek word *metanoia*, which we usually translate as "conversion" or "repentance," means to turn around or change direction. Those on the journey toward God's Kingdom must be willing to ask for directions if we are ever to find the way. Without a willingness to change, starting a life of prayer will be fruitless.

✢ *The Gift of Clear Sight* ✢

The first step in making certain that you pray honestly is to accept that you are a sinner. "If we say that we have no sin, we deceive ourselves, and the truth is not in us" (1 John 1:8). Prayer and repentance go together. You cannot offer yourself to God if you do not see yourself as you really are. You need God's help to see what needs to change, and then you need His help to change it. The ability to see yourself clearly is a gift from God, and you must ask Him for it.

The second step is to recognize that God already knows what you are, and loves you anyway! We have Jesus' death on the Cross as proof of that. Our problem is that we often find it hard to love ourselves as we are, so we assume that God doesn't love us either. We hold back the bad parts, so that our prayer is neither as bold nor as honest as it should be. We underestimate the depth of His love. This is tragic, because prayer is the intimate conversation of lovers, in which any kind of deceit is inexcusable. Genuine relationships cannot be based upon lies. If we do not offer ourselves to God honestly, as we are, there is no relationship!

❧ *Finding the Words* ❦

A lack of candor in our prayers can sometimes be detected in the words we use. Prayer should be conversational rather than pious, but we often use holy-sounding words that do not accurately reflect what we feel. The church's worship is solemn and formal, with language to fit the occasion. When we worship, we are transcending the life of the world, not reading the minutes of the previous meeting, and the words we use should reflect that.

But personal prayer is different. It is a one-on-one encounter with the One closest to you. Praying in the language of worship can sound downright strange. At dinner, you would not say, "I pray thee, pass thou the mustard," unless you *want* people to think you're weird. Speaking that way as a child to your Father sounds as if you are speaking through a stained-glass window. Express yourself honestly and openly. Do not pray like this: "O Lord, Thy parish council shall meet this evening to guide Thy flock, smitten with financial insecurity. We ask that Thou wouldst grant unto us wisdom to seek new sources of abundance for Thy people, that we may continue to praise and glorify Thy Holy Name. Amen." Yuck!

God must have a sense of humor, or He would have stopped listening a long time ago. It would be better to say, "God, this church has financial trouble and we need Your help." That is an honest statement of what you feel.

Prayer is the time when we should really open up to God. Cloaking our problems with false piety makes us sound silly and pompous. If we are using our stained-glass voice to cover up requests that are personal, and perhaps selfish, we are really off the mark. God is not stupid. He will see through what we are doing.

The key to talking with the Father is given us by the prayer used by His Son. The model Jesus gave the disciples begins, "Our Father," but in the language of the time, the word used meant "Daddy." It was a term of intimate endearment. The disciples must have been mightily confused. For centuries the Jews had believed God's name to be so holy that it could not even be spoken, and now Jesus tells them to call God "Dad." Now *that* is up-close and personal.

Remember, Jesus said that if we were to be converted, we had to become like children. Until life teaches them otherwise, children are often frank, to the point of brashness. And Jesus gives as a model *that* kind of direct simplicity. St. Paul reminds us of our status. "We cry out, 'Abba, Father.' The Spirit Himself bears witness with our spirit that we are children of God, and if children, then heirs—heirs of God and joint heirs with Christ" (Romans 8:16, 17). When we were baptized, the Father formally adopted us as sons and daughters, making Jesus our older brother. In baptism, God gave us the same kind of relationship that He has with His Son.

So make use of a good thing! God will not be shocked by the bluntness or frantic nature of any request. He may be the *only* one who will not be. If there is something eating at you, get it out, raw and undigested. He will listen to anything you have to say.

❧ *Are We Worthy?* ❧

No! We need to face up to that in prayer. If we are not willing to look closely at our sins and imperfections, we should never ask God for anything. I don't mean we must be canonized saints in order to pray, but we must practice self-examination to see if we are on track. Remember that we must "bear fruit to God" (Romans 7:4). We are supposed to show some change for the better in our lives.

This is no different from you telling your children, "You can go to the ball game if your room is picked up and the dishes are done. And don't forget to feed the dog." There is no free lunch. We expect our children to exercise responsibility if they want privileges. That is exactly what God wants His children to do. We exercise responsibility by making progress in the spiritual life, or as the Bible puts it, "bearing fruit." "But the fruit of the Spirit is love, joy, peace, longsuffering, kindness, goodness, faithfulness, gentleness, self-control" (Galatians 5:22, 23). God gives us a list of attributes His children are to develop. This will happen as the result of the Holy Spirit's action within us—and our cooperation with that Spirit. You do not have to be perfect in all these things, but you should at least be trying, and confessing when you fail. If we are not trying, it is really dishonest to make requests of God. I don't mean He will not listen in times of crisis, but that means we have an even greater responsibility to begin acting according to His will.

Most times, we know when we are doing wrong and when we

are not. When we are doing wrong and we try to pray, we resort to camouflage. Do you find yourself saying "we" when what you really mean is "I"? Are you making bargains with God—"If You heal my mother, I will go to church more"? Have you thrown in a lot of "Thy will be done," when what you actually are demanding is that *your* will be done? These are danger signs that warn us to start looking at ourselves before we start asking of God. Remember those words from Romans, "He who searches the hearts" (Romans 8:27). God already knows what is behind our words, so we may as well face it ourselves.

Approaching God honestly means examining how you are living and what you are praying for. We can always approach God without fear of rejection. He will listen to the frankest statements made directly from our hearts, including all those things that we find too embarrassing to say to others. How sad it is that we often are programmed to mistrust even God. We miss out on our best support. We will never pray effectively until we look at ourselves honestly, accept ourselves for what we are, and openly offer that to God.

Chapter 7

Meditation

I will meditate on Your precepts,
And contemplate Your ways.
—Psalm 119:15

Meditation is badly misunderstood. To many Christians, it sounds like something practiced by an elite corps of religious professionals, with powers far beyond those of mortal men.

The idea of meditation has also had some bad press. When I was in college (we will *not* mention how long ago that was), there was a great deal of interest in meditation, but it was from the pagan religions of the East that people took their inspiration. Movements like Transcendental Meditation and Krishna Consciousness were very popular. Young people who had been raised as Christians were attracted to these religions because they helped fill a spiritual need that, tragically, need never have existed.

Christianity, both Eastern and Western, has a rich tradition of meditation as part of a normal spiritual life. But Western Christianity, caught up in social activism or doctrinal pluralism, has ceased to present traditional teaching on the spiritual life in any popular form. Those who might have become the ascetics of today have been sidetracked into seeking real depth elsewhere. You cannot embrace what does not exist. So Christians either try to adapt essentially unchristian spiritualities, not knowing their own tradition, or, becoming members of pagan religions, many followers of the Lord turn their backs upon the source of Life.

Meditation is a part of the spiritual tradition and it should be a part of your prayer life. Meditation is not beyond your ability, regardless of your educational background or status in life. If you are serious about your prayer life, meditation must play a part in it.

Establishing our basic discipline is the most important part of beginning the life of prayer. At first we pray for short periods of time, but as we become more experienced, we will spend more time in prayer, and then meditation will start to play a role. We have seen the importance of being focused in quiet before starting our prayers. Meditation is an extension of this. Meditation can both prepare us and aid us in prayer.

Basically, meditation is prayerful thought—the application of our minds to understanding God's ways. "Make me understand the way of Your precepts; / So shall I meditate on Your wondrous works" (Psalm 119:27). Biblically, knowledge of God is not an end in itself, but a means of union with Him. God teaches His people how to love Him, and one of the ways we love Him is to try to understand that teaching.

I have mentioned the connection between love and relationship, even as it applies to God. When you love someone, you want to know him or her as much as possible. Meditation is an act of love that increases our knowledge of our Beloved. Jesus said, "If you love Me, keep My commandments" (John 14:15). In Psalm 119:2, we read, "Blessed *are* those who keep His testimonies, / Who seek Him with the whole heart!" It is our whole-hearted desire for God that leads us to prayerful thinking about who He is.

In meditation, we want to reflect as deeply as possible. While prayer is heartfelt conversation, meditation involves our minds to a greater degree. It brings more of us to the relationship. And it is precisely that involvement of the intellect that can put some people off. Believing our relationship with God to be completely spontaneous and emotional, they see meditation as choking off feeling.

Our feelings are an important part of our life in God, but they need a keeper. If prayer is based only on our emotions, it will be chaotic, unfocused, and ineffective. Because our aim is to pray effectively, we need the discipline that thoughtfulness brings. And God doesn't love us just for our bodies—He wants our minds as well!

In the writings of the Holy Fathers, we find a concept called the *nous*. This is a Greek word that is difficult to translate into English. Literally it means the "eye of the heart." It is often translated as "mind" or "intellect," and although its meaning is a bit more subtle than that, mind or intellect will serve for our purpose here. It is important to remember that sin does not just affect our bodies. The Fall involves the heart, soul, and mind (*nous*). All three of these parts of our being need to be purified and redeemed. In other words, we should be concerned not only about acting righteously, but about thinking righteously as well. Christian living cannot be a case of "clean mind, clean body: take your choice."

Remember what was said about intrusive thoughts? Sin begins in the mind, and if we do not cut it off there, our thoughts can lead to sin, even if it is only mental sin. Thinking about killing someone can be just as destructive to our salvation as actually killing. It darkens our thought, making it hard to think in a godly way. Meditation is a tool to help purify our minds, along with our souls and bodies.

As we grow in prayer, the line between meditation and prayer may not be all that clear. We may pass from speaking to reflecting and back again. When you meditate, you may be drawn by the Spirit into prayer, in which case you should pray. On the other hand, during prayer, we may be drawn back into thinking in order to understand what we are trying to say, so we move back into meditation. There is not, and should not be, any hard-and-fast distinction between prayer and meditation; on the contrary, they should be complementary.

No two people are alike. In the spiritual life, there are "different strokes for different folks." Some relate to God intellectually, others emotionally. We can bring the mind and the heart—intellect and feelings—closer together through both meditation and prayer. As the thinking person learns to use his feelings, and the feeling person his mind, each develops a greater spiritual wholeness.

Meditation is an act by which we reach out to God with our minds. In the Orthodox baptismal service, the believer is described as being a "reason-endowed sheep in the flock of Christ." For those who believe that no *nous* is good *nous*, let me say: We were never meant to check our brains at the door to our prayer closet.

Meditation is not preaching a sermon to ourselves or idly musing. It is purposefully coming to grips with the mystery that God is. This will not be dissection of God—exposing everything that He is—but an attempt to understand the way of His precepts.

❖ *From Self to God* ❖

The more we come to know God, the more we will know that we are His, and only His. It is just as possible for us to be possessed by ourselves as it is for us to be possessed by any demon. Given the human ego and our pridefulness, this may be a greater problem than the demons. How often do we see ourselves as being the center of a small, fixed universe in which everything revolves around us?

Meditation, used as a tool for learning God's ways, can help open a way out of that self-centered universe to an expanding reality. We will move beyond the point at which we are aware primarily of ourselves, and become more aware of God. His life and love will become the context of our life. Learning His will, and doing it, will become our most important activity. Meditation and prayer that do not lead to purposeful action are useless.

✣ *Begin at the Beginning* ✣

Because we are different from one another, there is probably no one way to meditate. There are, however, several ways we should avoid. Scrupulosity can be as much a problem in meditation as it is in prayer. It can bind us with anxiety over the "right way to do it." But the same basic rules we apply to prayer will help keep our effort focused on meditation.

Being quiet and undistracted is obviously necessary. Also, we must allow the Holy Spirit to direct us, even if He doesn't follow our game plan. There are several ways in which we may meditate. Perhaps you are interested in nature. Thinking about the mystery of God's creation, our place in it, or how we can exercise proper stewardship of it can be fruitful. It might lead us to think about Jesus' entry into His own creation for our salvation, and what this means for our response.

Or you may have a different turn of mind. I have one parishioner who tells me that he is closest to God when working on technical equipment. As I am not so inclined, this does nothing for me, but if he can see God in the workings of a computer chip, fine.

✣ *Sacred Reading* ✣

One way of meditating is sacred reading—the Bible, the Lives of the Saints, or sound theology, depending on your interests.

Sacred reading was practiced in the Middle Ages and was a required part of monastic life, as outlined in the Holy Rule of St.
Benedict. Called *lectio divina* in Latin, this was a slow, meditative
style of reading. A text, either from the Bible or the Fathers, would
be read slowly and thoughtfully. It was common to read out loud,
which sounds somewhat odd to us, until we think about how we
memorize something. Usually we read it aloud over and over until
we remember it. This is certainly one good way of reading scrip-
tural texts. Whether you read out loud or not, read slowly, paus-
ing frequently to think about what you have read, seeking to
engage the text with your heart and mind. Pray about what you
are reading, asking God to lead you to understanding.

Do not make the mistake of arguing with or dissecting what
you are reading. You should be concentrating on God, not
wondering why Jesus said what He did. Avoid unprofitable
diversion.

✦ *A Plug for the Psalms* ✦

One of the best ways to do sacred reading is to make use of the
Psalms. Many things that we can read will be helpful and instructive, but the Psalms are in a league of their own. The Psalms can
be used for oral prayer as well, especially during dry periods. These
are words inspired by God, and God will speak through them to us!

St. Athanasius described the Psalms as a mirror, meaning that
everything we can possibly feel is expressed in them and reflected
back to us. "And so, on the whole, each psalm is both spoken and
composed by the Spirit so that in these same words . . . the stirrings
of our souls might be grasped, and all of them said as concerning
us, and the same issue from us as our own words, for a remembrance of the emotions in us, and a chastening of our life" (St.
Athanasius, *Letter to Marcellinus*).

We can gain insight into many of our spiritual problems by

meditating upon the words of the Psalms. We can be comforted by the fact that what is happening to us is not unique. Do you feel in need of confession? Then read Psalm 51. Psalm 32 expresses the joy we feel in the forgiveness we receive after confession. Have you often wondered about the injustice of the world, in which the good suffer and the evil do not? So did the writer of Psalm 73. Do you feel surrounded by enemies, with no one to understand you? Turn to Psalm 140.

As in any meditation, do not argue with the thoughts expressed, or wonder about the person who wrote them. Just let those words become your words! Absorb them. They will help you express feelings that you may never be able to put into words. As the words become your words, rejoice in the knowledge that "the Spirit Himself bears witness with our spirit" (Romans 8:16). By using the spirit of the Psalms, we can learn just how much God shares with us, and we with Him.

❧ *The Sounds of Silence* ❧

Contemplative silence is the atmosphere necessary for meditation. At the risk of overemphasizing the point, silence is an essential element for all our spiritual activity. We live in a noisy world. Most of the noise that assaults us is useless, but even so it is pervasive and inescapable. Elevators, airports, shopping malls, and even workplaces have ever-present background music. If you are as easily distracted as I am, this can be a problem—it is as if the world does not want us to concentrate on God.

We have become so used to the noise that its absence can be disconcerting. Look at the way people tiptoe around in libraries—the silence seems oppressive, and we cannot wait to get out and make some noise.

Yet silence is necessary for hearing God, either in meditation or in prayer. God is persistent, but He will not usually force

Himself on us. So we must learn to listen. We can learn from an experience that Elijah had on Mt. Horeb. He was running from his enemies and encountered God.

> And behold, the Lord passed by, and a great and strong wind tore into the mountains and broke the rocks in pieces before the Lord, *but* the Lord *was* not in the wind; and after the wind an earthquake, *but* the Lord *was* not in the earthquake; and after the earthquake a fire, *but* the Lord *was* not in the fire; and after the fire **a still small voice**. (1 Kings 19:11, 12, emphasis added)

God is the still small voice. You must be quiet if you want to hear Him.

Of course it would be helpful if God would just show up sometime with a big "G" on His sweatshirt, so that we would know when to pay attention; but that is not His style. So we must listen for the small quiet voice, in silence. Try to empty your mind of distracting thoughts and images. This is not always easy, since nature—and Satan—abhor a vacuum.

Sit in front of your icon corner and enjoy the quiet presence of God. If you practice the Jesus Prayer, this can provide a background that protects against intrusive thoughts. Other than that, do not consciously try to pray or even meditate. "But he who is joined to the Lord is one spirit *with Him*" (1 Corinthians 6:17). Allow the Spirit to work; listen for God.

Contemplation is in God's control, not yours, so don't try to create an experience! It is possible that God wants to reveal something to you. With Paul, we may feel like one caught up into heaven. We may not know if we are in the body or out of it. Or our experience may be very simple and direct—just the quiet affirmation of God's presence and love. Treasure the experience and do not try to analyze it. Treat it as the shared intimacy between lovers that it is.

Your meditations may become simpler as you become more experienced. Sharing one thought with God could occupy hours. Your meditation may be fruitful in several ways: it will provide a good starting point for your prayers, or you may be given a flash of insight that you did not have before. It will provide the slowly growing knowledge of God that gives substance to our prayers. But none of this means that meditation is an end in itself. As such, it has no place in the Orthodox tradition. It is but one more tool to help you pray effectively.

Chapter 8

Signs Along the Way

The glory I know and I say it is Your
Holy Spirit. . . . But while I was there
surrounded by darkness, you appeared as
light.
—Simeon the New Theologian

If you faithfully follow a disciplined life of prayer, you will make progress; things will begin to happen to you spiritually. God always responds to sincere effort. Here I should tell you some of the things that can happen, and how you should respond. Some things are more important than others.

The first result of your increased effort may be a feeling of warm well-being—a sense that you are pulling yourself together. This is nice, but nothing to get too excited about. It is usually the result of the mechanics of concentration, and does not, in itself, represent spiritual growth. You need to be discerning, avoiding hasty conclusions as to how far you have come. You can produce the same kind of feeling by sitting cross-legged on the floor and chanting a Hindu mantra. In other words, this feeling is mechanically caused, not Spirit-directed.

There is the danger that you will mistake feelings for growth and become sidetracked, enjoying the feeling so much that you forget about prayer. Always remember that the purpose of prayer is not to have good feelings, but to learn the Father's will, and to share yourself with Him. This is a trap that I can guarantee people will fall into again and again. Faith means going forward in the firm conviction that God is working for the best, regardless of how you feel. There will be many times that you will have to act on that conviction, when all you want is a warm, fuzzy glow to convince you that God is real.

Beware! Satan can counterfeit anything, including good feelings. That is why the Orthodox tradition cautions so much against being too concerned about feelings. Does this mean we should feel bad about feeling good? Not at all! Just don't put too much trust in feelings; they are a poor indicator of how effective your prayer is.

✦ A Growing Presence ✦

The next stage may be a heightened awareness of God's presence and a greater sense of our own sinfulness, coupled with a deeper sense of devotion. Everything in our lives is seen more clearly, as if we were looking through new glasses for the first time. The clearness is the result of our own ascetical effort, rather than a gift of grace. Whenever we truly turn toward God, our awareness of His presence will be greater, and as the day follows night, we will become more aware of how spiritually impoverished our lives really are. If we are really seeking God, this awareness will spur us on to greater effort, marked by deeper devotion.

So far, so good. But this is not the sign of a great breakthrough. God is just being God—something that He is very good at—and we find Him. Our spiritual senses may quicken, but this is still prayer on a simple level. It will provide a foundation for deeper experience, an experience that cannot be forced and will come about only as God wills. You must still work at your praying, with God responding as He knows is appropriate.

This saying should remind us of how important our effort is: There is no such thing as a free lunch. God is always there, but we must respond to His presence. St. Theophan the Recluse writes:

> The help of God is always ready, and always near, but is only given to those who seek and work, and only to those seekers who, after putting all their own powers to the test, then cry out with all their heart: Lord, help us.

Some Christians believe that anything that smacks of discipline and concerted effort quenches the Spirit, but they are wrong. Without ascetical effort and spiritual struggle, there is no growth. The lives of the saints make it clear that only by overcoming our sins and passions can we purify ourselves enough so that God can really work in us. Never fall for the teaching that all you have to do is accept Jesus and everything moves forward by itself.

❧ Mirages in the Desert ❧

One of the purposes of prayer is to learn God's will in order to act on it. A logical question is, "How can we know what God's will is?" Or, to put it another way, how can we tell the difference between illusion and reality? And trust me: illusion, whether the result of enemy attack or of our own foolishness, will be a problem.

How nice it would be if, during our journey toward heaven, we came to a sign saying, "Only twenty more miles to the New Jerusalem. Restaurant and souvenir shops." Occasionally someone thinks he has seen just such a sign, and starts making plans to spend the night. Anyone who has ever traveled through a desert knows just how deceptive a mirage can be—like that patch of water on the road that you see but never seem to reach. When we want to see something badly enough, we usually see it. This is the power of illusion, or to use a more appropriate word, delusion. Whether its origin is in the devil's work or within yourself, illusion can lead us, in God's name, into ungodly activity. Scripture reminds us to test the spirits, to see if they are from God.

One way that you can tell delusion from reality is by its fruit. God will never ask you to do anything that is immoral (or fattening). If you feel urged to act in such a way, the prompting is not from God. But what if God seems to be telling us to do something good? How can we tell if it is really God speaking?

First, look at the possible results of the message received. God does not normally put a pipe upside our head, but He is direct. He does not inform us by sneaking into the back door of our consciousness. Satan, on the other hand, is always sneaky, because the only way he can win is by deceit. God loves us freely and openly. The devil slips us a Mickey, and then seduces us.

If we find ourselves overwhelmed by doubt and fear in response to some supposed prompting from God, it is probably not from Him. "Illusion is always met at first by a certain doubt in the heart; only those whom it has conquered decisively accept it without question" (St. Theophan the Recluse). We may be overcome with awe by the things God calls us to do, and we may doubt our ability to carry out His will, but God will never give us a spirit of fear. "There is no fear in love; but perfect love casts out fear" (1 John 4:18). Remember also that God will never ask us to do anything beyond what He knows is our strength.

If doubt and fear continue, you are probably dealing with an illusion. Acting on God's will results in a quiet confidence. You may have to deal with struggles outside of yourself, but interiorly there will be a calm that comes from being led by God, rather than charmed by illusion.

❖ *Breakthroughs* ❖

God has made us all with a wonderful diversity, each person having his own unique personality and gifts. But sometimes those differences can cause confusion in the life of prayer. Because we are different as people, my experiences of God may be different from yours. When dealing with each person, God concentrates on that person's own particular needs. My encounter is no better or worse than yours, but it may be different.

Sometimes we long for something dramatic to happen, just to prove that what is going on is real—perhaps like the experience Paul had on the Damascus road. "As he journeyed he came near Damascus, and suddenly a light shone around him from heaven. Then he fell to the ground, and heard a voice saying to him, 'Saul, Saul, why are you persecuting Me?'" (Acts 9:3, 4).

Now, something like that gets your attention! But Paul was a hard-case persecutor of the Church who needed a heavy two-by-four to get his attention. That doesn't mean you do. On the contrary, a desire for that kind of attention from God actually reveals a lust for spiritual experience rather than a desire for God. Rest assured that if God has an experience with your name on it, you will have it. If not, don't worry that your spirituality is not "real." Do not assume that because someone you know has been "knocked off his horse," he is further along than you are. He might just be more stubborn than you. And remember, never judge spirituality by feelings.

❖ *Inexpressible Words* ❖

When you do read about those who have had profound spiritual experiences, you may be struck by the restraint they use in describing them. The saints were not in the business of boasting about themselves. Since it is difficult to express heavenly realities in human language, holy experiences can be difficult to put into words. Some of the images used in the writings of the saints can sound simplistic and naive at best. Or they may be maddeningly vague.

> I know a man in Christ who fourteen years ago—whether in the body I do not know, or whether out of the body I do not know, God knows—such a one was caught up to the third heaven. And I know such a man—whether in the body or out of the body I do not know, God knows— how he was caught up into Paradise and heard inexpressible words, which it is not lawful for a man to utter. (2 Corinthians 12:2–4)

This was written by the same Paul God "nailed" outside Damascus. Who knows if he is speaking of himself or someone else. But later on he gives a hint that he is describing his own vision, although it is still hard to tell from the way he writes. He mentions being caught up into Paradise and hearing things that should not be spoken of. This was undoubtedly a mystical experience, but Paul seems to have trouble putting it into words. And he is adamant that "of such a one I will boast; yet of myself I will not boast, except in my infirmities" (2 Corinthians 12:5).

Paul, like all the saints, did not hang his experiences out there for others to marvel at. Paul is afraid that his readers will think he is boasting, so he tries hard to make it clear there is no reason for him to do so. This shows us two things: first, genuine spiritual experience is not easily packaged for mass consumption. Second, we should be careful how we share this kind of intimate experience with others, lest we become victims of pride and vainglory. If you have had a deep experience, it might be helpful to share it with a fellow struggler, but only as God directs you to do so. You could do much harm by provoking someone who doesn't have such experiences into despair and innocently providing Satan with a way to trip you up.

Remember that even good things can be used against you, which is another reason we must have good spiritual direction. Trying to make sense out of spiritual experience can be quite frustrating, because you are too close to the event. God is far beyond your ability to fully describe and explain, especially to yourself. In order to understand a spiritual breakthrough, you need guidance. And remember that, as with Elijah, an experience may be quiet, but nonetheless profound.

❖ Learning the Language ❖

Learning to pray effectively is like any other skill—you must know the jargon that goes with the trade. The writings of those who have been tested in the spiritual life—those we call saints—can be of great value, when combined with good spiritual direction. There are now good English translations of many Orthodox spiritual writings, and selections from them, such as the *Philokalia*. We may still need help interpreting them, but a lack of material will not be a problem. Personally, I believe it is helpful to read the Tradition as it developed; along with the Bible, start reading the sayings of the Desert Fathers, and then read your way through spiritual history. Ask your spiritual father or mother for help in this.

One thing that these writings will help you to understand is the basis for the Orthodox teaching of deification, which is seen as the goal of spiritual life. We are called to become *like* God, but we do not *become* God. And no matter how holy we do become, we will never see God the Father as He is. In other words, we will never completely comprehend Him.

Moses had a close relationship with God. The Lord spoke to Moses "face to face, as a man speaks to his friend" (Exodus 33:11). That would be a nice kind of relationship to have, and you might think Moses would be content with that. But one day, he decided to push things a bit. He asked to see God in His glory, and so the Father had to sit Moses down and explain the rules of the game to him:

> Then He said, "I will make all My goodness pass before you, and I will proclaim the name of the Lord before you. . . ." But He said, "You cannot see My face; for no man shall see Me, and live." And the Lord said, "Here is a place by Me, and you shall stand on the rock. So it shall be, while My glory passes by, that I will put you in the cleft of the rock, and will cover you with My hand while I pass by. Then I will take away My hand, and you shall see My back; but My face shall not be seen" (Exodus 33:19–23).

Now this does seem a bit contradictory; they speak face to face, but no one can see God's face. Even in the Psalms, God says, "Seek My face" (Psalm 27:8). As we said, explaining the reality of heaven with earthly words can be tricky, and it can lead to some first-class misunderstanding. Biblical imagery can be very plastic, leading to different meanings depending on context. God and Moses had a familiar relationship based on regular communication. Hence they spoke "face to face"—frequent and close communication.

What Moses asked for, and what we sometimes ask for, was to see God's glory—to see God as He is. In theological terms, Moses wanted to see God's "essence." This we cannot do. We do see God's face in His Son, who is the express image, in the creation, of the Father. God does tell Moses that he can see His back after the fullness of His divine glory passes by, which sounds a bit weird. But it makes a point.

In commenting on this, St. Gregory of Nyssa wrote, "He who desires to behold God sees the object of his longing in always following Him." In this sense, there is never a point at which you catch up to God, because there is always more mystery about Him to discover. He always leads us to deeper experience.

But the passage in which God answers Moses' request is also pointing out that we will not encounter Him in His essence as God, but in that part of Him that spills over into the creation. The Orthodox term is "energies." The distinction between God's essence and His energies is important for understanding Orthodox spirituality. God's essence is His very nature; the energies are the power that comes from His nature as God. All of us have power to move, to think, to act.

God's essence is what He is: pure, uncreated being—life so dynamic and full as to be beyond human ability to comprehend. In a sense it could be dangerous. Coming into contact with God's essence could drive us mad, if not destroy us. Any follower of *Star Trek* knows what happens when matter and antimatter come into contact. God's existence is so superabundantly perfect that it is antimatter to our matter. We could not endure it.

But God is so full of creative, dynamic life that it is constantly spilling over into the creation. The power that comes from His nature, and that comes into the creation from Him, we call God's energies. It is much like the corona of the sun, which we can see only during an eclipse—great sprouts of fire leaping out into space. God's energies are not specially created by God, but are just part of Him, and these energies we may experience in various ways.

❖ *A Light in the Dark* ❖

God is often described in terms of light. Jesus said, "I am the light of the world. He who follows Me shall not walk in darkness, but have the light of life" (John 8:12). At the Transfiguration (Luke 9:28–36), Jesus shone with the uncreated Light of God, and even Moses came down from Mt. Sinai with his face shining from the presence of God (Exodus 34:29).

Yet the presence of the same God has been experienced as darkness. Moses encountered darkness on Mt. Sinai. This chapter began with a quote from St. Simeon the New Theologian, who describes an encounter with God in terms of both darkness and light.

Our first encounter will probably be with light—in other words, God, as our senses can perceive Him. Jesus is the Light of the world, because in Him we encounter the perfect expression, in human form, of God's presence in His creation.

When Philip asks Jesus to show the Father to the disciples, Jesus responds, "Have I been with you so long, and yet you have not known Me, Philip? He who has seen Me has seen the Father; so how can you say, 'Show us the Father'?" (John 14:9). When the Bible refers to seeing the face of God, it means the face of Christ. We meet the Father in the Son.

Meeting God in light means experiencing Him in comprehensible terms: "That which was from the beginning, which we have heard, which we have seen with our eyes, which we have looked upon, and our hands have handled" (1 John 1:1). In other words, we experience God in light in all the ways in which it was possible for God to manifest Himself in the creation, and that we can experience with our senses, from the burning bush to His Incarnate Son.

When we begin our spiritual lives, we will experience God in this way—hence the feelings of warmth and well-being already described. He shows Himself to us in concrete ways such as bread and wine, oil and incense, feeling and thought. As long as this creation is the context in which we encounter God, it is the concrete things that will be pivotal. For example, there will never be a time, this side of heaven, when we will outgrow the need to take Holy Communion.

But as you grow and progress, God will offer experiences that take us beyond the realm of easy definition. In his book, *The Life of Moses*, St. Gregory of Nyssa describes it this way:

> For leaving behind everything that is observed, not only what sense comprehends but also what the intelligence thinks it sees, it keeps on penetrating deeper until by the intelligence's yearning for understanding it gains access to the invisible and incomprehensible, and there it sees God.

There will come a point at which God asks us to walk ahead into the unknown, leaving behind us every prop and support we have, in an action of complete faith—in a sense, going beyond faith itself. We will have to trust God enough to meet Him without the familiar footholds and handholds. It will be as if God takes us to the edge of a cliff, surrounded by fog, and says, "Just step off, please." So we take a deep breath and walk out into the dark.

Entering that darkness means approaching that which is beyond all sense and all knowledge. Because we are now beyond all that is familiar and comfortable, we feel as if we were in the dark. But because God is there, it is a luminous darkness that shows the Divine Presence.

You see how difficult it can be to put into words? The experience is so much more than we can describe. We fumble for words, knowing that we can never communicate clearly the absolute joy of going further into God. Perhaps it is best not to try. Those who have been there will know what you mean without being told. Those who have not yet been there will not yet understand.

And we will return to the old familiar places. Growth and understanding will continue to take place in real, normal places. Now they will have new meaning, as we learn what it is to live in two worlds at once: the world of sense and sight and sound; and the world of "Mount Zion . . . the city of the living God, the heavenly Jerusalem, to an innumerable company of angels" (Hebrews 12:22).

The life of the Church encompasses both earth and heaven. We are only travelers in this visible creation, for our true home is in heaven. And that is why we strive to be detached from the things of this world—not because they are bad, but because they are only a means to an end. They sustain us along the Way, but they are not themselves the Way. St. Paul reminds us that "our citizenship is in heaven" (Philippians 3:20). If there is so little growth in so many Christians' lives, is it not because we have become comfortable in a world that is only a shadow of that which is to come? We have settled for too little.

The more you orient yourself toward God, the more you experience heavenly reality, and the more you will understand that you must continue moving forward. If you come to feel as if you have one foot here and one foot beyond—good! All is as it should be.

Chapter 9

Wrapping Up

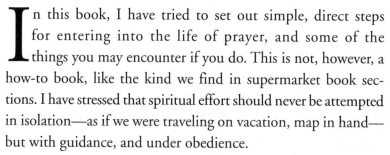

In this book, I have tried to set out simple, direct steps for entering into the life of prayer, and some of the things you may encounter if you do. This is not, however, a how-to book, like the kind we find in supermarket book sections. I have stressed that spiritual effort should never be attempted in isolation—as if we were traveling on vacation, map in hand—but with guidance, and under obedience.

If you want to deepen your prayer life, then, the first thing you must do is to speak with your pastor. He is the one that God has placed spiritually over you, and if you are to be directed by someone else, you need his blessing. He can also recommend reading that will be helpful. One thing that must be discussed is your pastor's role in guiding your spiritual life. He may be quite comfortable with doing so, or he may not, but probably he can suggest someone who can. If he refuses to fulfill this role, do not take it personally. He may simply be too busy with pastoral duties to give the attention that spiritual direction serves.

Perhaps you live near an Orthodox monastery, either of men or women, and there you have an even greater resource. For centuries, Orthodox Christians have received spiritual guidance from holy men and women who have embraced the monastic life. In North America, monasticism is not the strong presence that it has been in other parts of the Orthodox world, but the situation is improving, and more Americans are responding to the monastic call. In addition to the possibility of finding a spiritual director, a monastery provides the quiet, undisturbed atmosphere that is necessary for spiritual effort. Although you may not live there, you can visit, taking part in the services, receiving the sacraments, and soaking up some good atmosphere. Whether or not your spiritual director is attached to the monastery, it is still a good place for prayer, retreat, and contemplation.

✦ Praying in a Group ✦

The life of prayer can be a real struggle, and all of us who attempt it need the help and support of others, especially if they share the same struggle. A support group of people who are engaged in active prayer lives, and understand the problems we face, can be a real help. It may be that there are like-minded people in your congregation who can help you in your effort, and whom you may help as well. (Your pastor can help put you in touch with them.)

Prayer is personal conversation with God, not group therapy, so I am not suggesting you try to form the kind of prayer group that exists in many Protestant churches. There, members come together to share prayer and concerns in a group meeting, which may include hymn-singing and very personal expressions of piety and commitment. This does not fit in well with Orthodox spirituality. It has no biblical model, whereas we have seen Jesus give very explicit instructions about "going into our room" and "speaking to our Father in secret." The prayer group dynamic is often heavy on emotion and warm feelings, and very short on sound doctrine. In fact, the group can become so important, or its leader so dominant, that it becomes a substitute for the normal worship of the community.

But there is no reason why Orthodox Christians cannot get together to pray some of the short liturgical services known as the Hours, or even a simplified form of Vespers. I have mentioned the importance of daily worship—in addition to daily prayer—in the life of an Orthodox Christian. Some churches offer the daily services, and others, for various reasons, do not; if your parish does not, then you need to fill that gap somehow. We can pray the Hours by ourselves without too much trouble, and there are forms for lay Vespers and Matins which would not take much instruction to perform. But if you are the only person doing it, either at home or in the church building, it can become burdensome and frustrating. If the pastor gives his permission, there is no reason why this offering cannot be shared with others for mutual encouragement and support—if not daily, then several times per week.

For example, in the Antiochian Orthodox Archdiocese of North America, the St. Philip's Prayer Fellowship is a group of people all over the country who share a common rule of discipline and prayer. A prayerbook is published with prayers and services. There are many other such books printed by other Orthodox Christian groups that include forms for morning and evening prayers, as well as small liturgical services. You can pray these at home, knowing that you are joined in a common offering with others; or it may be possible to gather with people from your own congregation. If you desire to make intercessions for others or for certain needs, it should be done in accordance with the prayers that are given for that purpose, and not by sharing information or feelings about a person or situation with the group.

However, you can become a source of intercession and spiritual support for your church. Too many of our parishes and missions lack a real sense of depth and direction, and I believe this may be because there is so little praying that goes on in them, or on the congregation's behalf. We must pray for our pastors and staffs, offering them up before God, asking Him to strengthen and direct them in their work, and keeping them in our hearts. It is possible that this kind of praying group, gathering on a regular basis, could become a faithful remnant, a spiritual leaven in a parish, transforming the life of the congregation. There should be no sense of elitism or egocentrism in this. This group is not more special because they pray together or share spiritual goals. They should receive no extraordinary recognition. But they may, by example, call others to a more disciplined, deeper spiritual life, and this leads to spiritual growth in the congregation. They can offer on behalf of others what the others may not have the time, or the understanding, to offer up to God.

✤ *Prayer in Public Places* ✦

Something should be said about the Orthodox attitude toward some of the discussions about prayer taking place in our society: praying publicly in schools, at the flagpole, and in other public venues. Where I live, in the American South, we have prayers before high school sports events and school activities, with few people batting an eye. (This is sometimes done in opposition to what the court system allows.) At this time, in my state, a bill is working its way through the legislature over the issue of whether or not people can pray in the public school system. How should an Orthodox Christian respond?

I would never question the sincerity or devotion of those who wish to do these things, but there are some legitimate questions that need to be addressed from an Orthodox perspective. We believe that there is a biblical model of how we should pray, and to whom prayer is addressed. Orthodox Christians believe in the Holy Trinity, God being three Persons sharing one essence: Father, Son, and Holy Spirit, One God. He is always Trinity. There are not times when He is just the Father, or just the Son, or just the Holy Spirit. It is important to have prayer rooted in sound belief, because what we believe can affect how we pray, and vice versa. Many of the prayers that we hear offered in public are not prayers based upon the realization of God's Triune Nature.

Orthodox prayer is offered to the Father, through the Son, in the Holy Spirit. We are involved with all three Persons of the Holy Trinity when we pray, but in specific ways. If you look at Orthodox worship prayers, and even the private prayers that we find in the devotional books, this is how they are written. Jesus begins the Lord's Prayer with "Our Father," the Father being the object of our praying. Jesus is the One who has gained access for us to the Father by His death, Resurrection, and Ascension into heaven. We pray to the Father through and with Him. The Holy Spirit, as we remember from Paul's Epistle to the Romans, prays through us, the spirit of prayer joining with our spirit. A prayer that is not shaped according to this model, however sincerely offered, does not adequately reflect who God is.

As for the issue of prayers offered in school or other public places, we do need to remember Jesus' teaching about where we should pray. He said to go into our room, not our homeroom. You can, of course, be in prayer anywhere, and given the biblical teaching that we should "pray without ceasing," we should be praying everywhere. The Jesus Prayer, and other forms of prayer such as "Lord, have mercy," can be offered any time, anywhere, as often as possible. Certainly you can talk conversationally to God anywhere as well, although you might want to be careful about who can overhear you. Doing this in psychology class could lead to a referral to the school counselor.

But we need to be careful what kinds of policies we try to put into practice that can affect others. Because we are sympathetic to fellow believers, we may wind up pushing forms of prayer that not only are not Orthodox, but are of such a bland, inoffensive nature as to be virtually non-Christian as well. God is not glorified by this. Certainly these prayers should never be seen as a substitute for the kind of disciplined praying that the spiritual life requires. Remember that we are told to "pray in secret." Outside of worship, prayer is meant to be an intimate experience with our Father, and intimacy can be hard to achieve when the marching band is waiting to play "The Star-Spangled Banner" and the cheerleaders are waiting to run onto the field.

In addition, we live in an increasingly pluralistic society, made up of people who not only come from different areas of the world, but hold different religions and worldviews. At the time of this writing, there may be more Moslems living in the United States than Jews. There is a Buddhist temple not far from my home, and there may be a Hindu temple not far from yours. Previously, most immigrants came from places that had been shaped in some way by Western culture and were within the Judeo-Christian tradition, but this is no longer the case. However one may feel about this, it is a fact, and it is not going to change.

It is possible, therefore, in an area in which there has been a large immigration from Southeast Asia, that a majority of students in a school may be Buddhists. Presumably there is a City Council somewhere that is made up of Moslems or Mormons. There is one small town, only about twenty miles from mine, which was founded and is populated by people who are actively involved in the occult. What kinds of prayers or spirituality would we like to have them impose upon us?

Many Christians are used to thinking of the government as some kind of ally, but in biblical times and beyond, it was seen as no such thing. When Paul wrote, "Therefore I exhort first of all that supplications, prayers, intercessions, and giving of thanks be made for all men, for kings and all who are in authority, that we may lead a quiet and peaceable life in all godliness and reverence" (1 Timothy 2:1), he was not writing of praying for Christians in government—there were none. At best the civil authorities may have been Jews, but mostly likely they were pagans who would have believed in God-only-knows-what. But the apostle still says to pray for them, so "that we may lead a quiet and peaceable life." In other words, keep them off our backs, God, and don't let them interfere in our lives too much.

The government was something to be kept neutral, so that Christians could appeal to it when they were wronged—as Paul appealed to have his case heard by the Roman emperor—but not have an alien faith imposed on them by it, as so often happened. Later, as Christianity became a legal religion, the situation changed and an alliance was formed between Church and State, which lead to great good but also to great problems. Christians in power don't seem to handle it better than anyone else. There has been interference from the State in the life of the Church, and even embarrassing times of persecution of Christians *by* Christians when they have had the State to back them up.

Church/State issues are difficult to work through, especially when one group depends on the government to hold up its side. The early Christian sense of neutrality is probably a better way to go. This doesn't mean that you cannot have the Ten Commandments in public buildings, for example—our legal system has been shaped by such things—but it does mean that we should avoid imposing on others, in the name of religious fervor, what Christians have never wanted imposed on them.

For the Orthodox Christian, spirituality cannot be imposed from the outside, but must spring from our innermost desire for union with God. All of our ascetic struggle, all of our praying, all of our longing must have as its goal knowing Him, loving Him, and seeking to do His will.

Other Books of Interest from Conciliar Press

Ascending the Heights, by Fr. John Mack

In the sixth century, a monk named John wrote a book outlining the stages of the spiritual life. He based his entire work on the image of a ladder of thirty rungs, stretching from earth to heaven. Each rung described a step in the pursuit of virtue and the spiritual life. Since it was first written, *The Ladder of Divine Ascent* has been an essential part of the formation of Orthodox monastics, and a mainstay of Orthodox ascetic spirituality. But it is not just for monks and nuns.

Fr. John Mack wrote this book to help those in a nonmonastic setting understand how to apply *The Ladder of Divine Ascent* to their lives. Each chapter contains many direct quotes from St. John's writings, in addition to commentary on St. John's words. This book, therefore, should be used as a primer to the Ladder—as a helpful tool for ascending the spiritual heights. Paperback, 156 pages (ISBN 1-888212-17-9) Order No. 004729— $14.95

The Jesus Prayer: A Gift from the Fathers, by Fr. David Hester

"O Lord Jesus Christ, Son of God, have mercy on me." This prayer has been on the lips of Christians since the time of the Desert Fathers. What is its history? How do we make it our own? This booklet traces the development of the Jesus Prayer through the early centuries of the Church, and follows its progression through Mount Athos, the teachings of St. Gregory Palamas, and others, and discusses its modern revival in the 19th and 20th centuries. Concludes with a brief discussion of how this prayer can be appropriated by the individual believer today. 32-page booklet (ISBN 1-888212-26-8) Order No. 005213—$3.50

Seasons of Grace: Reflections on the Church Year
by Donna Farley

Why do feasts and seasons matter? There is beauty and grace in the cycle of the church year, but sometimes we don't understand its significance to us. These short yet thoughtful reflections, written in an insightful and sometimes humorous style, will help weave together the great feasts into the fabric of our lives. Paperback (ISBN 1-888212-50-0) Order No. 005658–$14.95

Turning the Heart to God, by St. Theophan the Recluse
translated by Fr. Kenneth Kaisch and Igumen Iona Zhiltsov
 One of the most profound works on repentance in all of Christendom.
St. Theophan, a beloved Orthodox bishop from nineteenth-century Russia,
speaks not only from a deep knowledge of the Church Fathers, but also from
a lifetime of experience in turning his heart to God—and guiding others on
this glorious Way that leads to our salvation. His writings are unique in that
he combines centuries of Church wisdom with keen psychological insights
for us today.
 Repentance is not a popular term here in the West, yet it is the corner-
stone of the Lord's gospel, and the entrance into God's kingdom. *Turning the
Heart to God* is a manual of true spiritual transformation in a world of often
cheap grace . . . a classic book that has the power to change our lives, if we let
it. Paperback, 176 pages (ISBN 1-888212-22-5) Order No. 005064—$13.95

The Unseen Warfare Series

 Father Jack Sparks has masterfully adapted the material from this highly
treasured monastic work specifically for today's lay Christian living in the
midst of a modern world. The result is a profound but highly practical resource for those who seek to strive with all their might against the enemies of
our souls—the world, the flesh, and the devil. Study questions at the end of
each chapter facilitate individual or small group study.
 Victory, Virtue, and Prayer are complementary in content, but do not
overlap. Can be read separately or as a set.
Victory in the Unseen Warfare (0-9622713-6-5) Order No. 001001 —$10.95
Virtue in the Unseen Warfare (0-9622713-8-1) Order No. 001002 —$10.95
Prayer in the Unseen Warfare (1-888212-03-9) Order No. 002269—$10.95
Save 20% when ordering the UNSEEN WARFARE SET (1-888212-05-5)
Order No. 002823—price for set of all 3 books, $27.95

Note: Prices listed were current as of February, 2003, but are subject to change.
Prices do not include sales tax or postage & handling.

To request a Conciliar Press catalog of other books
about the Orthodox Faith and church life,
to place a credit card order, or to obtain current ordering information,
please call Conciliar Press at (800) 967-7377 or (831) 336-5118,
or log on to our website: www.conciliarpress.com